Teacher's Guide 3
Composition Skills

Author: Chris Whitney

William Collins' dream of knowledge for all began with the publication of his first book in 1819.

A self-educated mill worker, he not only enriched millions of lives, but also founded a flourishing publishing house. Today, staying true to this spirit, Collins books are packed with inspiration, innovation and practical expertise. They place you at the centre of a world of possibility and give you exactly what you need to explore it.

Collins. Freedom to teach.

Published by Collins
An imprint of HarperCollins*Publishers*
The News Building
1 London Bridge Street
London
SE1 9GF

Browse the complete Collins catalogue at
www.collins.co.uk

© HarperCollins*Publishers* Limited 2017

10 9 8 7 6 5 4 3

ISBN 978-0-00-822304-5

British Library Cataloguing in Publication Data

A catalogue record for this publication is available from the British Library.

Publishing Director: Lee Newman
Publishing Manager: Helen Doran
Senior Editor: Hannah Dove
Project Manager: Emily Hooton
Author: Chris Whitney
Development Editors: Robert Anderson and Sarah Snashall
Copy-editor: Tanya Solomons
Proofreader: Cicely Thomas and Tracy Thomas
Cover design and artwork: Amparo Barrera and Ken Vail Graphic Design
Internal design concept: Amparo Barrera
Typesetter: Ken Vail Graphic Design
Production Controller: Rachel Weaver

Printed and bound by CPI Group (UK) Ltd, Croydon, CR0 4YY

Acknowledgements

The publishers wish to thank the following for permission to reproduce content. Every effort has been made to trace copyright holders and to obtain their permission for the use of copyright materials. The publishers will gladly receive any information enabling them to rectify any error or omission at the first opportunity.

Extracts on pages 23-24 from *The King in the Forest* by Michael Morpurgo, Hodder Childrens Books, 2001, pp.5-8, copyright © 1993 Michael Morpurgo. Reproduced with permission of Hachette Children's Books, Carmelite House, 50 Victoria Embankment, London EC4Y 0DZ.

Contents

About Treasure House

Treasure House is a comprehensive and flexible bank of books and online resources for teaching the English curriculum. The Treasure House series offers two different pathways: one covering each English strand discretely (Skills Focus Pathway) and one integrating texts and the strands to create a programme of study (Integrated English Pathway). This Teacher's Guide is part of the Skills Focus Pathway.

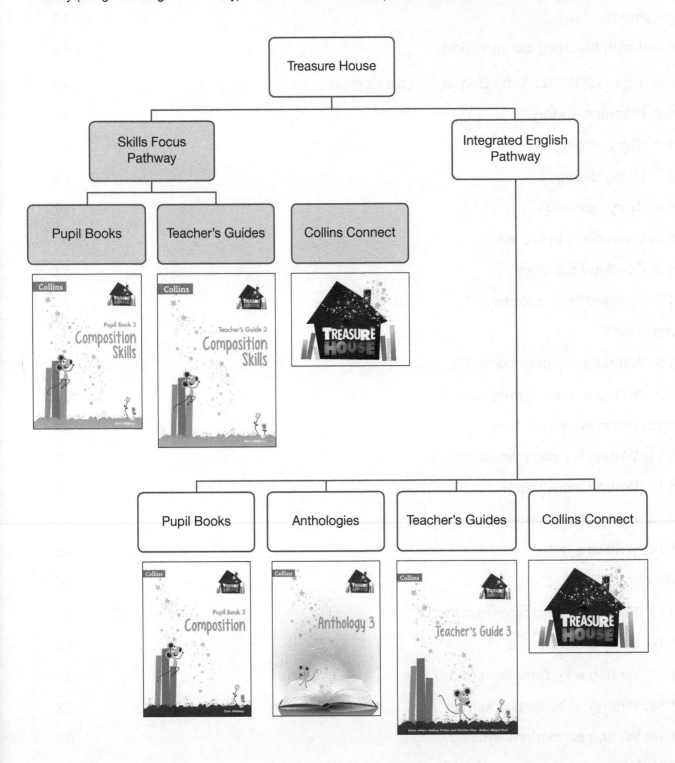

1. Skills Focus

The Skills Focus Pupil Books and Teacher's Guides for all four strands (Comprehension; Spelling; Composition; and Vocabulary, Grammar and Punctuation) allow you to teach each curriculum area in a targeted way. Each unit in the Pupil Book is mapped directly to the statutory requirements of the National Curriculum. Each Teacher's Guide provides step-by-step instructions to guide you through the Pupil Book activities and digital Collins Connect resources for each competency. With a clear focus on skills and clearly-listed curriculum objectives you can select the appropriate resources to support your lessons.

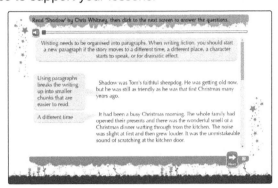

2. Integrated English

Alternatively, the Integrated English pathway offers a complete programme of genre-based teaching sequences. There is one Teacher's Guide and one Anthology for each year group. Each Teacher's Guide provides 15 teaching sequences focused on different genres of text such as fairy tales, letters and newspaper articles. The Anthologies contain the classic texts, fiction, non-fiction and poetry required for each sequence. Each sequence also weaves together all four dimensions of the National Curriculum for English – Comprehension; Spelling; Composition; and Vocabulary, Grammar and Punctuation – into a complete English programme. The Pupil Books and Collins Connect provide targeted explanation of key points and practice activities organised by strand. This programme provides 30 weeks of teaching inspiration.

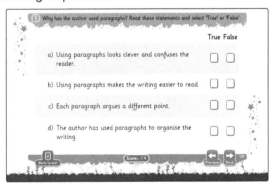

Other components

Handwriting Books, Handwriting Workbooks, Word Books and the online digital resources on Collins Connect are suitable for use with both pathways.

Treasure House Skills Focus Teacher's Guides

Year	Comprehension	Composition	Vocabulary, Grammar and Punctuation	Spelling
1	978-0-00-822290-1	978-0-00-822302-1	978-0-00-822296-3	978-0-00-822308-3
2	978-0-00-822291-8	978-0-00-822303-8	978-0-00-822297-0	978-0-00-822309-0
3	978-0-00-822292-5	978-0-00-822304-5	978-0-00-822298-7	978-0-00-822310-6
4	978-0-00-822293-2	978-0-00-822305-2	978-0-00-822299-4	978-0-00-822311-3
5	978-0-00-822294-9	978-0-00-822306-9	978-0-00-822300-7	978-0-00-822312-0
6	978-0-00-822295-6	978-0-00-822307-6	978-0-00-822301-4	978-0-00-822313-7

Inside the Skills Focus Teacher's Guides

The teaching notes in each unit in the Teacher's Guide provide you with subject information or background, a range of whole class and differentiated activities including photocopiable resource sheets and links to the Pupil Book and the online Collins Connect activities.

Each **Overview** provides clear objectives for each lesson tied into the new curriculum, links to the other relevant components and a list of any additional resources required.

Teaching overview provides a brief introduction to the specific skill concept or text type and some pointers on how to approach it.

Support, embed & challenge supports a mastery approach with activities provided at three levels.

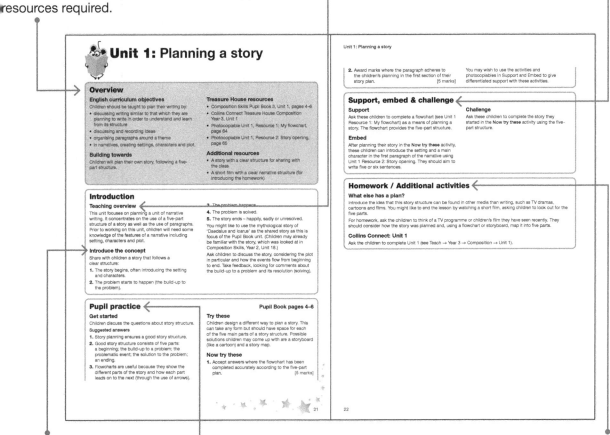

Introduce the concept/text provides 5–10 minutes of preliminary discussion points or class/group activities to get the pupils engaged in the lesson focus and set out any essential prior learning.

Pupil practice gives guidance and the answers to each of the three sections in the Pupil Book: *Get started*, *Try these* and *Now try these*.

Homework / Additional activities lists ideas for classroom or homework activities, and relevant activities from Collins Connect.

Two photocopiable **resource** worksheets per unit provide differentiated support for the writing task in each lesson. They are designed to be used with the activities in support or embed sections.

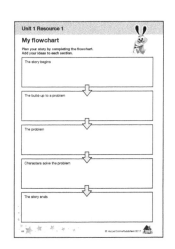

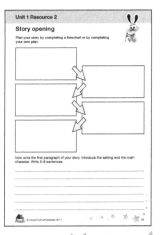

Treasure House Skills Focus Pupil Books

There are four Skills Focus Pupil Books for each year group, based on the four dimensions of the National Curriculum for English: Comprehension; Spelling; Composition; and Vocabulary, Grammar and Punctuation. The Pupil Books provide a child-friendly introduction to each subject and a range of initial activities for independent pupil-led learning. A Review unit for each term assesses pupils' progress.

Year	Comprehension	Composition	Vocabulary, Grammar and Punctuation	Spelling
1	978-0-00-823634-2	978-0-00-823646-5	978-0-00-823640-3	978-0-00-823652-6
2	978-0-00-823635-9	978-0-00-823647-2	978-0-00-823641-0	978-0-00-823653-3
3	978-0-00-823636-6	978-0-00-823648-9	978-0-00-823642-7	978-0-00-823654-0
4	978-0-00-823637-3	978-0-00-823649-6	978-0-00-823643-4	978-0-00-823655-7
5	978-0-00-823638-0	978-0-00-823650-2	978-0-00-823644-1	978-0-00-823656-4
6	978-0-00-823639-7	978-0-00-823651-9	978-0-00-823645-8	978-0-00-823657-1

Inside the Skills Focus Pupil Books

Comprehension

Includes high-quality text extracts covering poetry, prose, traditional tales, playscripts and non-fiction.

Pupils retrieve and record information, learn to draw inferences from texts and increase their familiarity with a wide range of literary genres.

Composition

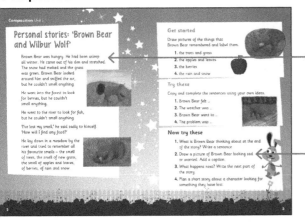

Includes high-quality, annotated text extracts as models for different types of writing.

Children learn how to write effectively and for a purpose.

Vocabulary, Grammar and Punctuation

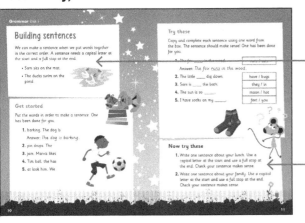

Develops children's knowledge and understanding of grammar and punctuation skills.

A rule is introduced and explained. Children are given lots of opportunities to practise using it.

Spelling

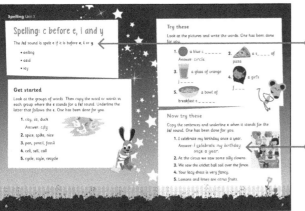

Spelling rules are introduced and explained.

Practice is provided for spotting and using the spelling rules, correcting misspelt words and using the words in context.

Treasure House on Collins Connect

Digital resources for Treasure House are available on Collins Connect which provides a wealth of interactive activities. Treasure House is organised into six core areas on Collins Connect:

- Comprehension
- Spelling
- Composition
- Vocabulary, Grammar and Punctuation
- The Reading Attic
- Teacher's Guides and Anthologies.

For most units in the Skills Focus Pupil Books, there is an accompanying Collins Connect unit focused on the same teaching objective. These fun, independent activities can be used for initial pupil-led learning, or for further practice using a different learning environment. Either way, with Collins Connect, you have a wealth of questions to help children embed their learning.

Treasure House on Collins Connect is available via subscription at connect.collins.co.uk

Features of Treasure House on Collins Connect

The digital resources enhance children's comprehension, spelling, composition, and vocabulary, grammar, punctuation skills through providing:

- a bank of varied and engaging interactive activities so children can practise their skills independently
- audio support to help children access the texts and activities
- auto-mark functionality so children receive instant feedback and have the opportunity to repeat tasks.

Teachers benefit from useful resources and time-saving tools including:

- teacher-facing materials such as audio and explanations for front-of-class teaching or pupil-led learning
- lesson starter videos for some Composition units
- downloadable teaching notes for all online activities
- downloadable teaching notes for Skills Focus and Integrated English pathways
- the option to assign homework activities to your classes
- class records to monitor progress.

Comprehension

- Includes high-quality text extracts covering poetry, prose, traditional tales, playscripts and non-fiction.
- Audio function supports children to access the text and the activities

Composition

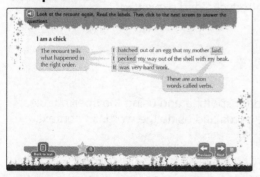

- Activities support children to develop and build more sophisticated sentence structures.
- Every unit ends with a longer piece of writing that can be submitted to the teacher for marking.

Vocabulary, Grammar and Punctuation

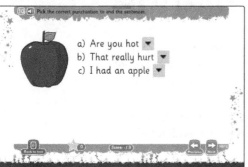

- Fun, practical activities develop children's knowledge and understanding of grammar and punctuation skills.
- Each skill is reinforced with a huge, varied bank of practice questions.

Spelling

- Fun, practical activities develop children's knowledge and understanding of each spelling rule.
- Each rule is reinforced with a huge, varied bank of practice questions.
- Children spell words using an audio prompt, write their own sentences and practise spelling using Look Say Cover Write Check.

Reading Attic

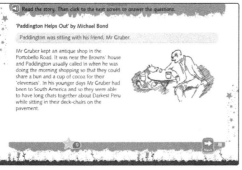

- Children's love of reading is nurtured with texts from exciting children's authors including Michael Bond, David Walliams and Michael Morpurgo.
- Lesson sequences accompany the texts, with drama opportunities and creative strategies for engaging children with key themes, characters and plots.
- Whole-book projects encourage reading for pleasure.

Treasure House Digital Teacher's Guides and Anthologies

The teaching sequences and anthology texts for each year group are included as a flexible bank of resources.

The teaching notes for each skill strand and year group are also included on Collins Connect.

Support, embed and challenge

Treasure House provides comprehensive, detailed differentiation at three levels to ensure that all children are able to access achievement. It is important that children master the basic skills before they go further in their learning. Children may make progress towards the standard at different speeds, with some not reaching it until the very end of the year.

In the Teacher's Guide, Support, Embed and Challenge sections allow teachers to keep the whole class focussed with no child left behind. Two photocopiable resources per unit offer additional material linked to the Support, Embed or Challenge sections.

Support

The Support section offers simpler or more scaffolded activities that will help learners who have not yet grasped specific concepts covered. Background information may also be provided to help children to contextualise learning. This enables children to make progress so that they can keep up with the class.

To help with children's composition skills, activities are broken down into smaller steps, for example, children draw pictures, write plans or complete templates before writing sentences.

If you have a teaching assistant, you may wish to ask him or her to help children work through these activities. You might then ask children who have completed these activities to progress to other more challenging tasks found in the Embed or Challenge sections – or you may decide more practice of the basics is required. Collins Connect can provide further activities.

Embed

The Embed section includes activities to embed learning and is aimed at those who children who are working at the expected standard. It ensures that learners have understood key teaching objectives for the age-group. These activities could be used by the whole class or groups, and most are appropriate for both teacher-led and independent work.

In Composition, children can practise their writing skills using templates, plans and prompts allowing them to write a variety of text-types at the required standard.

Challenge

The Challenge section provides additional tasks, questions or activities that will push children who have mastered the concept without difficulty. This keeps children motivated and allows them to gain a greater depth of understanding. You may wish to give these activities to fast finishers to work through independently.

In Composition, children's writing skills can be enhanced with the freer activities in the Challenge section, for example, they may write an alternative ending to a story, retell a story in their own words or think about a story from another perspective. Children can demonstrate more advanced use of vocabulary and manipulate grammar more accurately through these tasks.

Assessment

Teacher's Guide

There are opportunities for assessment throughout the Treasure House series. The teaching notes in Treasure House Teacher's Guides offer ideas for questions, informal assessment and spelling tests.

Pupil Book Review units

Each Pupil Book has three Review units designed as a quick formative assessment tool for the end of each term. Questions assess the work that has been covered over the previous units. These review units will provide you with an informal way of measuring your pupils' progress. You may wish to use these as Assessment for Learning to help you and your pupils to understand where they are in their learning journey.

In Treasure House, there is a strong focus on genres of texts that widen children's knowledge of writing for different purposes and audiences. In Composition, the review units allow children to demonstrate what they know in independent tasks. Vocabulary, grammar and punctuation can be assessed through their writing as well as their understanding of a genre.

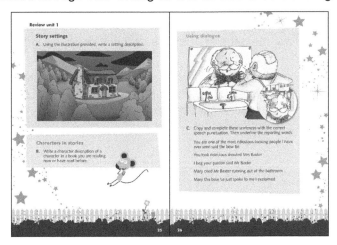

Assessment in Collins Connect

Activities on Collins Connect can also be used for effective assessment. Activities with auto-marking mean that if children answer incorrectly, they can make another attempt helping them to analyse their own work for mistakes. Homework activities can also be assigned to classes through Collins Connect. At the end of activities, children can select a smiley face to indicate how they found the task giving you useful feedback on any gaps in knowledge.

Class records on Collins Connect allow you to get an overview of children's progress with several features. You can choose to view records by unit, pupil or strand. By viewing detailed scores, you can view pupils' scores question by question in a clear table-format to help you establish areas where there might be particular strengths and weaknesses both class-wide and for individuals.

If you wish, you can also set mastery judgements (mastery achieved and exceeded, mastery achieved, mastery not yet achieved) to help see where your children need more help.

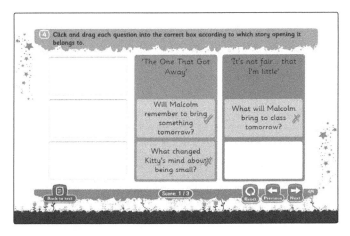

Support with teaching composition

Composition is one of the four core dimensions of the National Curriculum for English. Within the teaching of English, the aim is to ensure that all pupils write clearly, accurately and coherently, adapting their language and style in and for a range of contexts, purposes and audiences.

Effective composition involves forming, articulating and communicating ideas, and then organising them coherently for a reader. This requires clarity and an awareness of the audience, purpose and context. All children can be helped towards better writing if shown how to generate and organise ideas appropriately and how to then transfer them successfully from plan to page. In addition, pupils need to be taught how to plan, revise and evaluate their writing. These aspects of writing have been incorporated into the Treasure House Composition Skills strand.

Throughout the primary years, we want pupils to have opportunities to write for a range of real purposes and audiences as part of their work across the curriculum. These purposes and audiences should underpin the decisions about the form the writing should take, such as a narrative, an explanation or a description. We want pupils to develop positive attitudes towards their writing and stamina for it by writing narratives about personal experiences and those of others, by writing about real events, by writing poetry and by writing for different purposes.

Pupils also need to be taught to monitor whether their own writing makes sense. They should also understand, through being shown, the skills and processes essential for writing: the generation of ideas, initial drafting, and re-reading to check that the meaning is clear.

Treasure House Composition Skills Teacher's Guides provide extensive notes and guidance for teaching a range of genres and text types. The integrated pupil books provide opportunities for pupils to plan, draft and edit their writing. Each unit is linked to an extract of quality text from which the teaching ideas are taken.

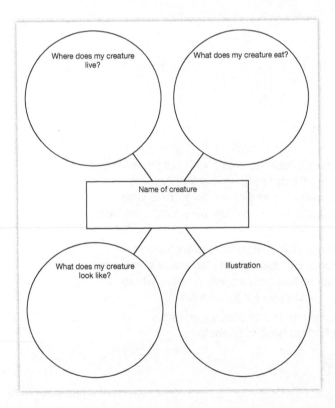

Flora

Write the next sentence in the story.

What happens to Flora? How does her story develop?

Draw a picture here.	Write the story.
Draw a picture here.	Write the story.
Draw a picture here.	Write the story.

Delivering the 2014 National Curriculum for English

Unit	Title	Treasure House Resources	Collins Connect	English Programme of Study
1	Planning a story	• Composition Skills Pupil Book 3, Unit 1, pages 4–6 • Composition Skills Teacher's Guide 3 – Unit 1, pages 21–22 – Photocopiable Unit 1, Resource 1: My flowchart, page 64 – Photocopiable Unit 1, Resource 2: Story opening, page 65	Collins Connect Treasure House Composition Year 3, Unit 1	**Writing:** Discussing writing similar to that which they are planning to write in order to understand and learn from its structure. Discussing and recording ideas. Organising paragraphs around a theme. In narratives, creating settings, characters and plot.
2	Story settings	• Composition Skills Pupil Book 3, Unit 2, pages 7–9 • Composition Skills Teacher's Guide 3 – Unit 2, pages 23–24 – Photocopiable Unit 2, Resource 1: My three story settings, page 66 – Photocopiable Unit 2, Resource 2: My story setting, page 67	Collins Connect Treasure House Composition Year 3, Unit 2	**Writing:** Discussing writing similar to that which they are planning to write in order to understand and learn from its structure. Organising paragraphs around a theme. In narratives, creating settings, characters and plot.
3	Using dialogue	• Composition Skills Pupil Book 3, Unit 3, pages 10–12 • Composition Skills Teacher's Guide 3 – Unit 3, pages 25–26 – Photocopiable Unit 3, Resource 1: Reporting words, page 68 – Photocopiable Unit 3, Resource 2: A dialogue between Mr Baxter and his friend, page 69	Collins Connect Treasure House Composition Year 3, Unit 3	**Writing:** Using and punctuating direct speech.
4	Story openings	• Composition Skills Pupil Book 3, Unit 4, pages 13–15 • Composition Skills Teacher's Guide 3 – Unit 4, pages 27–28 – Photocopiable Unit 4, Resource 1: Story openings – sentences, page 70 – Photocopiable Unit 4, Resource 2: Story openings – paragraph, page 71	Collins Connect Treasure House Composition Year 3, Unit 4	**Writing:** Discussing writing similar to that which they are planning to write in order to understand and learn from its structure. Discussing and recording ideas. Organising paragraphs around a theme. In narratives, creating settings, characters and plot.

Unit	Title	Treasure House Resources	Collins Connect	English Programme of Study
5	Characters in stories	• Composition Skills Pupil Book 3, Unit 5, pages 16–18 • Composition Skills Teacher's Guide 3 – Unit 5, pages 29–30 – Photocopiable Unit 5, Resource 1: My character, page 72 – Photocopiable Unit 5, Resource 2: Planning my character's story, page 73	Collins Connect Treasure House Composition Year 3, Unit 5	**Writing:** Discussing writing similar to that which they are planning to write in order to understand and learn from its structure. Organising paragraphs around a theme. In narratives, creating settings, characters and plot.
6	Continuing a story	• Composition Skills Pupil Book 3, Unit 6, pages 19–21 • Composition Skills Teacher's Guide 3 – Unit 6, pages 31–32 – Photocopiable Unit 6, Resource 1: Continuing a story: King Arthur, page 74 – Photocopiable Unit 6, Resource 2: Continuing a story: Merlin, page 75	Collins Connect Treasure House Composition Year 3, Unit 6	**Writing:** Discussing writing similar to that which they are planning to write in order to understand and learn from its structure. Organising paragraphs around a theme. In narratives, creating settings, characters and plot.
7	Paragraphs in stories	• Composition Skills Pupil Book 3, Unit 7, pages 22–24 • Composition Skills Teacher's Guide 3 – Unit 7, pages 33–34 – Photocopiable Unit 7, Resource 1: My new paragraph, page 76 – Photocopiable Unit 7, Resource 2: Paragraph checklist, page 77	Collins Connect Treasure House Composition Year 3, Unit 7	**Writing:** Composing and rehearsing sentences orally (including dialogue). Organising paragraphs around a theme. In narratives, creating settings, characters and plot.
8	Writing a rhyming poem (1)	• Composition Skills Pupil Book 3, Unit 8, pages 27–29 • Composition Skills Teacher's Guide 3 – Unit 8, pages 36–37 – Photocopiable Unit 8, Resource 1: My rhyming poem, page 78 – Photocopiable Unit 8, Resource 2: My season poem, page 79	Collins Connect Treasure House Composition Year 3, Unit 8	**Reading:** Listening to and discussing a wide range of fiction and poetry. Preparing poems and play scripts to read aloud and to perform, showing understanding through intonation, tone, volume and action. Recognising some different forms of poetry (for example, free verse, narrative poetry). **Writing:** Discussing writing similar to that which they are planning to write in order to understand and learn from its structure.

Unit	Title	Treasure House Resources	Collins Connect	English Programme of Study

9	Writing a non-rhyming poem	• Composition Skills Pupil Book 3, Unit 9, pages 30–32
		• Composition Skills Teacher's Guide 3
		  – Unit 9, pages 38–39
		  – Photocopiable Unit 9, Resource 1: My descriptive phrases, page 80
		  – Photocopiable Unit 9, Resource 2: From my window, page 81
			Collins Connect Treasure House Composition Year 3, Unit 9	**Reading:** Listening to and discussing a wide range of fiction and poetry.
				Preparing poems and play scripts to read aloud and to perform, showing understanding through intonation, tone, volume and action.
				Recognising some different forms of poetry (for example, free verse, narrative poetry).
				Writing: Discussing writing similar to that which they are planning to write in order to understand and learn from its structure.

10	Planning non-fiction	• Composition Skills Pupil Book 3, Unit 10, pages 33–35
		• Composition Skills Teacher's Guide 3
		  – Unit 10, pages 40–41
		  – Photocopiable Unit 10, Resource 1: Planning my report, page 82
		  – Photocopiable Unit 10, Resource 2: My report, page 83
			Collins Connect Treasure House Composition Year 3, Unit 10	**Writing:** Discussing writing similar to that which they are planning to write in order to understand and learn from its structure.
				Organising paragraphs around a theme.
				In non-narrative material, using simple organisational devices (for example, headings and sub-headings).

11	Writing an information text (1)	• Composition Skills Pupil Book 3, Unit 11, pages 36–38
		• Composition Skills Teacher's Guide 3
		  – Unit 11, pages 42–43
		  – Photocopiable Unit 11, Resource 1: Planning my report, page 84
		  – Photocopiable Unit 11, Resource 2: My report, page 85
			Collins Connect Treasure House Composition Year 3, Unit 11	**Writing:** Discussing writing similar to that which they are planning to write in order to understand and learn from its structure.
				Organising paragraphs around a theme.
				In non-narrative material, using simple organisational devices (for example, headings and sub-headings).

12	Writing instructions	• Composition Skills Pupil Book 3, Unit 12, pages 39–41
		• Composition Skills Teacher's Guide 3
		  – Unit 12, pages 44–45
		  – Photocopiable Unit 12, Resource 1: Getting ready to cook, page 86
		  – Photocopiable Unit 12, Resource 2: My recipe, page 87
			Collins Connect Treasure House Composition Year 3, Unit 12	**Writing:** Discussing writing similar to that which they are planning to write in order to understand and learn from its structure.
				In non-narrative material, using simple organisational devices (for example, headings and sub-headings).

Unit	Title	Treasure House Resources	Collins Connect	English Programme of Study
13	Paragraphs in non-fiction	• Composition Skills Pupil Book 3, Unit 13, pages 42–44 • Composition Skills Teacher's Guide 3 – Unit 13, pages 46–47 – Photocopiable Unit 13, Resource 1: My topic sentences, page 88 – Photocopiable Unit 13, Resource 2: My paragraphs, page 89	Collins Connect Treasure House Composition Year 3, Unit 13	**Writing:** Discussing writing similar to that which they are planning to write in order to understand and learn from its structure. Organising paragraphs around a theme. In non-narrative material, using simple organisational devices (for example, headings and sub-headings).
14	Writing a letter	• Composition Skills Pupil Book 3, Unit 14, pages 45–47 • Composition Skills Teacher's Guide 3 – Unit 14, pages 48–49 – Photocopiable Unit 14, Resource 1: Planning my letter, page 90 – Photocopiable Unit 14, Resource 2: My letter, page 91	Collins Connect Treasure House Composition Year 3, Unit 14	**Writing:** Discussing writing similar to that which they are planning to write in order to understand and learn from its structure. Organising paragraphs around a theme. In non-narrative material, using simple organisational devices (for example, headings and sub-headings).
15	Reviewing and proofreading	• Composition Skills Pupil Book 3, Unit 15, pages 50–52 • Composition Skills Teacher's Guide 3 – Unit 15, pages 51–52 – Photocopiable Unit 15, Resource 1: Planet Zig, page 92 – Photocopiable Unit 15, Resource 2: The new friend, page 93	Collins Connect Treasure House Composition Year 3, Unit 15	**Writing:** Evaluating and editing by assessing the effectiveness of their own and others' writing and suggesting improvements. Proposing changes to grammar and vocabulary to improve consistency including the accurate use of pronouns in sentences. Proofreading for spelling and punctuation errors.
16	Story plot	• Composition Skills Pupil Book 3, Unit 16, pages 53–54 • Composition Skills Teacher's Guide 3 – Unit 16, pages 53–54 – Photocopiable Unit 16, Resource 1: Flora, page 94 – Photocopiable Unit 16, Resource 2: Developing the plot, page 95		**Writing:** Discussing writing similar to that which they are planning to write in order to understand and learn from its structure. Discussing and recording ideas. Organising paragraphs around a theme. In narratives, creating settings, characters and plot.

Unit	Title	Treasure House Resources	Collins Connect	English Programme of Study
17	Writing an information text (2)	• Composition Skills Pupil Book 3, Unit 17, pages 55–56 • Composition Skills Teacher's Guide 3 – Unit 17, pages 55–56 – Photocopiable Unit 17, Resource 1: My poster, page 96 – Photocopiable Unit 17, Resource 2: My fact file, page 97		**Writing:** Discussing writing similar to that which they are planning to write in order to understand and learn from its structure. Organising paragraphs around a theme. In non-narrative material, using simple organisational devices (for example, headings and sub-headings).
18	Writing a rhyming poem (2)	• Composition Skills Pupil Book 3, Unit 18, pages 57–59 • Composition Skills Teacher's Guide 3 – Unit 18, pages 57–58 – Photocopiable Unit 18, Resource 1: A special memory, page 98 – Photocopiable Unit 18, Resource 2: Special memories, page 99		**Reading:** Listening to and discussing a wide range of fiction and poetry. Preparing poems and play scripts to read aloud and to perform, showing understanding through intonation, tone, volume and action. Recognising some different forms of poetry (for example, free verse, narrative poetry). **Writing:** Discussing writing similar to that which they are planning to write in order to understand and learn from its structure.
19	Writing an explanation text	• Composition Skills Pupil Book 3, Unit 19, pages 60–62 • Composition Skills Teacher's Guide 3 – Unit 19, pages 59–60 – Photocopiable Unit 19, Resource 1: Labelled flowchart, page 100 – Photocopiable Unit 19, Resource 2: Flowcharts with sentences, page 101		**Writing:** Discussing writing similar to that which they are planning to write in order to understand and learn from its structure. In non-narrative material, using simple organisational devices (for example, headings and sub-headings).

Unit	Title	Treasure House Resources	Collins Connect	English Programme of Study
20	Writing recounts	• Composition Skills Pupil Book 3, Unit 20, pages 63–65 • Composition Skills Teacher's Guide 3 – Unit 20, pages 61–62 – Photocopiable Unit 20, Resource 1: The Great Fire of London, page 102 – Photocopiable Unit 20, Resource 2: My history recount, page 103		**Writing:** Discussing writing similar to that which they are planning to write in order to understand and learn from its structure. Organising paragraphs around a theme. In narratives, creating settings, characters and plot. In non-narrative material, using simple organisational devices (for example, headings and sub-headings).
	All units	The following statutory requirements can be covered throughout the programme: Pupils should be taught to: • read aloud their own writing, to a group or the whole class, using appropriate intonation and controlling the tone and volume so that the meaning is clear.		

Unit 1: Planning a story

Overview

English curriculum objectives

Children should be taught to plan their writing by:

- discussing writing similar to that which they are planning to write in order to understand and learn from its structure
- discussing and recording ideas
- organising paragraphs around a theme
- in narratives, creating settings, characters and plot.

Building towards

Children will plan their own story, following a five-part structure.

Treasure House resources

- Composition Skills Pupil Book 3, Unit 1, pages 4–6
- Collins Connect Treasure House Composition Year 3, Unit 1
- Photocopiable Unit 1, Resource 1: My flowchart, page 64
- Photocopiable Unit 1, Resource 2: Story opening, page 65

Additional resources

- A story with a clear structure for sharing with the class
- A short film with a clear narrative structure (for introducing the homework)

Introduction

Teaching overview

This unit focuses on planning a unit of narrative writing. It concentrates on the use of a five-part structure of a story as well as the use of paragraphs. Prior to working on this unit, children will need some knowledge of the features of a narrative including setting, characters and plot.

Introduce the concept

Share with children a story that follows a clear structure:

1. The story begins, often introducing the setting and characters.
2. The problem starts to happen (the build-up to the problem).
3. The problem happens.
4. The problem is solved.
5. The story ends – happily, sadly or unresolved.

You might like to use the mythological story of 'Daedalus and Icarus' as the shared story as this is focus of the Pupil Book unit. (Children may already be familiar with the story, which was looked at in Composition Skills, Year 2, Unit 18.)

Ask children to discuss the story, considering the plot in particular and how the events flow from beginning to end. Take feedback, looking for comments about the build-up to a problem and its resolution (solving).

Pupil practice

Pupil Book pages 4–6

Get started

Children discuss the questions about story structure.

Suggested answers

1. Story planning ensures a good story structure.
2. Good story structure consists of five parts: a beginning; the build-up to a problem; the problematic event; the solution to the problem; an ending.
3. Flowcharts are useful because they show the different parts of the story and how each part leads on to the next (through the use of arrows).

Try these

Children design a different way to plan a story. This can take any form but should have space for each of the five main parts of a story structure. Possible solutions children may come up with are a storyboard (like a cartoon) and a story map.

Now try these

1. Accept answers where the flowchart has been completed accurately according to the five-part plan. [5 marks]

2. Award marks where the paragraph adheres to the children's planning in the first section of their story plan. [5 marks]

You may wish to use the activities and photocopiables in **Support and Embed** to give differentiated support with these activities.

Support, embed & challenge

Support

Ask these children to complete a flowchart (see Unit 1 Resource 1: My flowchart) as a means of planning a story. The flowchart provides the five-part structure.

Embed

After planning their story in the **Now try these** activity, these children can introduce the setting and a main character in the first paragraph of the narrative using Unit 1 Resource 2: Story opening. They should aim to write five or six sentences.

Challenge

Ask these children to complete the story they started in the **Now try these** activity using the five-part structure.

Homework / Additional activities

What else has a plan?

Introduce the idea that this story structure can be found in other media than writing, such as TV dramas, cartoons and films. You might like to end the lesson by watching a short film, asking children to look out for the five parts.

For homework, ask the children to think of a TV programme or children's film they have seen recently. They should consider how the story was planned and, using a flowchart or storyboard, map it into five parts.

Collins Connect: Unit 1

Ask the children to complete Unit 1 (see Teach → Year 3 → Composition → Unit 1).

Unit 2: Story settings

Overview

English curriculum objectives

Children should be taught to plan their writing by:

- discussing writing similar to that which they are planning to write
- organising paragraphs around a theme
- in narratives, creating settings, characters and plot.

Building towards

Children will plan and write their own story opening.

Treasure House resources

- Composition Skills Pupil Book 3, Unit 2, pages 7–9
- Collins Connect Treasure House Composition Year 3, Unit 2

- Photocopiable Unit 2, Resource 1: My three story settings, page 66
- Photocopiable Unit 2, Resource 2: My story setting, page 67

Additional resources

- A bank of stories with atmospheric settings for children to browse and explore
- A short film where the setting lends itself to discussion

Introduction

Teaching overview

This unit focuses on planning a story setting. It uses a text by the well-known British writer Michael Morpurgo, 'The King in the Forest', for analysis. Children read the extract and discuss the vocabulary used, the sensory quality of the writing and the atmosphere evoked, prior to writing their own setting. Children also consider how setting is evoked in film and compare it with how authors compose setting.

Michael Morpurgo (born 1943), the UK's Children Laureate in 2004, is best known for *War Horse* (1982).

Introduce the concept

Watch a film clip with a strong atmospheric setting and ask children to describe and discuss the setting (place) with their partners. Encourage them to talk about the following:

- In what kind of place is the story set? (inside/ outside; countryside/city; in a real place / in a fantastic place (for example, another planet), and so on)
- What does the director show? (for example, rooms, buildings, mountains, a whole planet!)

- How does he or she show it? (for example, in close-up / using a panning shot; at night / in the daytime; with music / natural sounds)

Take feedback.

Discuss with children how writers only have words to describe a setting (though illustrations can help). Ask children to consider what authors do in order to make settings vivid in the reader's eye. They could consider the book they are reading at the time, or one of the books from the selection you have brought in, and reflect on the setting in that book. Ideas might include:

- describing the setting literally – a 'list' of what is there
- describing the setting in sensory terms – in terms of the senses (for example, mostly sights, sounds and smells, but also what things feel like or even taste like)
- the use of similes and metaphors to make descriptions more vivid.

Explain that they will be writing their own settings after further discussion.

Pupil practice

Pupil Book pages 7–9

Get started

Children read the extract and then answer questions about the setting in the extract, considering the techniques used by the author. They may work in pairs discussing the answers prior to writing them.

Answers

1. The setting is a forest in a land ruled by a king in an unspecified medieval/fairy tale time period.   [1 mark]

2. A white fawn (something 'white and small' moving at the edge of the forest); the huntsmen riding.
[1 mark for each point]

3. The sound of hunting horns echoing; the baying of the hounds.   [1 mark for each point]

Children's lists may not match these exactly. They may also list things that have been described (such as the cow and the donkey) as sights, which is acceptable. Children should be encouraged to look only at what is actually in the text, rather than what they assume they would see and hear in a forest.

Try these

Accept any appropriate adjectives, giving one mark for each. Allow for unusual and creative choices.
[1 mark for each acceptable adjective]

Now try these

1. Children come up with different story settings and give a summary description for each.

2. Children choose a setting and write a description. Accept paragraphs that use descriptive language to bring the scene to life. The writing should show a sensory approach as well as descriptive language.

You may wish to use the activities and photocopiables in **Support and Embed** to give differentiated support with these activities.

Support, embed & challenge

Support

Ask the children to use Unit 2 Resource 1: My three story settings to draw three different settings and label them with descriptive noun phrases. They write a descriptive sentence for one of them. This replaces **Now try these** question 2.

Embed

Ask the children to use Unit 2 Resource 2: My story setting to write their description of a setting chosen from three provided in the **Now try these** activity. They are expected to use the techniques learned from analysis of the extract in their own writing. They should discuss these with a partner prior to writing.

Challenge

Ask the children to consider how the description they chose in the **Now try these** activity could form the setting for a longer narrative. They plan (using the techniques practised in Unit 1) and write their story.

Homework / Additional activities

Setting the scene

Ask the children to write a description of a room in their home. They should remember to describe the sights, the sounds and the smells as well as telling us what is in the room. They may draw a picture also. They should bring their descriptions to school to share with the class.

Collins Connect: Unit 2

Ask the children to complete Unit 2 (see Teach → Year 3 → Composition → Unit 2).

Unit 3: Using dialogue

Overview

English curriculum objectives

- Year 3 children should be taught to use and punctuate direct speech.

Building towards

Children will write a short dialogue, with correct punctuation and using reporting words.

Treasure House resources

- Composition Skills Pupil Book 3, Unit 3, pages 10–12
- Collins Connect Treasure House Composition Year 3, Unit 3

- Photocopiable Unit 3, Resource 1: Reporting words, page 68
- Photocopiable Unit 3, Resource 2: A dialogue between Mr Baxter and his friend, page 69

Additional resources

- A bank of stories that include dialogue for children to browse and read
- A short film clip in which two characters speak to each other

Introduction

Teaching overview

This unit focuses on the use of dialogue in a narrative setting and stresses the importance of dialogue to move the action forwards and to develop characters. It also covers the important rules children should learn when including dialogue in their stories.

This unit teaches these rules through analysis of a short extract taken from 'The Talking Bow Tie' by the Australian writer Morris Lurie (1938–2014), who is especially well known for his comic short stories.

Introduce the concept

Watch a film clip where two characters talk to each other. Ask children to watch what the camera does and to think about how the viewer knows who is talking. The aim is to get children to see that the camera is pointed towards the person who is speaking and then moves to capture the face of the second person speaking. Ask: 'If this is how it works in film, then how do we know who is speaking in written text?' Ask children to discuss this and take feedback.

To help us know when people are talking and who is talking, stories use:

- speech marks at the start and end of spoken words
- a capital letter at the start of the speech
- punctuation (a comma, full stop, question mark or exclamation mark) before the closing speech marks
- a new line for each new speaker
- reporting verbs (for example, 'Joe said', 'Anna shouted', 'he/she/I mumbled').

Read the text together. Ask the children to locate the speech and associated punctuation. Ask volunteers to read the words spoken by Mr Baxter and the bow tie.

Pupil practice

Pupil Book pages 10–12

Get started

Children discuss the questions with a partner and then write answers where required.

Answers

1. It is important to use speech marks to separate the dialogue and narrative. [1 mark]

2. Put speech marks at the start and end of spoken word; put a capital letter at the start of the speech; start a new line for each new speaker; punctuate the speech before the closing speech marks; use reporting words. [1 mark for each point]

3. Accept all possible substitutes for 'said'. [1 mark for each reporting word]

Try these

The children punctuate the sentences, using the dialogue in the text as a model.

Answers

1. "I thought I'd wear it tonight," said Mr Baxter. [1 mark]

2. "Oh, very lovely!" said Mrs Baxter. [1 mark]

3. "You don't look very smart," said the bow tie. [1 mark]

4. "You should be ashamed of yourself," cried Mrs Brown. [1 mark]

5. "It was me," he said quietly. "I stole the biscuits." [1 mark]

6. Jenny breathed a sigh of relief. "Thank goodness!" [1 mark]

7. "Roll up! Roll up!" shouted the man in the top hat. [1 mark]

8. I will shake her by the hand and say, "Thank you!" [1 mark]

Now try these

Suggested answers

1. Accept correctly punctuated and spelt sentences including a reporting word.

2. Accept a dialogue appropriate to the text, which is correctly punctuated and uses reporting words.

You may wish to use the activities and photocopiables in **Support and Embed** to give differentiated support with these activities.

Support, embed & challenge

Support

Ask the children to decide on five reporting words and write them in a list on Unit 3 Resource 1: Reporting words, which provides support for a shorter version of **Now try these** question 1. Then ask them to use the words in sentences, checking for accurate punctuation of speech and correct spelling of the reporting words.

Embed

Ask the children to use Unit 3 Resource 2: A dialogue between Mr Baxter and his friend to complete **Now try these** question 2. Ask the children to write a few lines including dialogue in which Mr Baxter tells his friend about the talking bow tie. The children are supported in this by the prompts provided.

Challenge

Ask these children to continue the story from the extract. Mr and Mrs Baxter are going out to dinner. What happens at the dinner table in the restaurant when Mr Baxter's bow tie begins to talk? Children should remember to include dialogue and to punctuate it correctly.

Homework / Additional activities

Listen and write

Ask the children to listen to a conversation at home – perhaps a conversation over the dinner table or on the sofa. They should capture this in a short piece of dialogue and check that it is punctuated correctly. They should attempt to use a variety of reporting words.

Collins Connect: Unit 3

Ask the children to complete Unit 3 (see Teach → Year 3 → Composition → Unit 3).

Unit 4: Story openings

Overview

English curriculum objectives

Year 3 Children should be taught to plan their writing by:

- discussing writing similar to that which they are planning to write in order to understand and learn from its structure
- discussing and recording ideas
- organising paragraphs around a theme
- in narratives, creating settings, characters and plot.

Building towards

Children will plan and write their own story opening.

Treasure House resources

- Composition Skills Pupil Book 3, Unit 4, pages 13–15
- Collins Connect Treasure House Composition Year 3, Unit 1
- Photocopiable Unit 4, Resource 1: Story openings – sentences, page 70
- Photocopiable Unit 4, Resource 2: Story openings – paragraph, page 71

Additional resources

- A bank of well-known stories that open in different ways

Introduction

Teaching overview

This unit focuses on story openings. There are many different ways to open stories, many of which are discussed in the unit. Some stories start with action and some with dialogue. Others begin by describing the setting or the main character. Some may even begin by asking a question. Children should understand that the opening draws in the reader and for this reason needs to be planned carefully.

The unit asks children to compare and contrast two story openings – one by Jan Mark (1943–2006) and the other by Bel Mooney (born 1946) – both set in a school.

Introduce the concept

Ask children to share with their partner the opening of the book they are currently reading. Ask them to compare and then discuss how the two stories differ in the way they open. Ask: 'Do they share any similarities?'

Come together as a group to discuss what you have found as a class and create a spider diagram of the different ways in which stories can open, for example:

- right in the middle of the action
- with dialogue that sets the scene
- with a description of a character
- with a description of a setting
- with a startling statement
- with an attention-grabbing question.

Share some openings from well-known stories and discuss them in the light of the class findings. Which kind of opening makes the children want to read on?

Explain to the children that they will be reading two different openings in the extracts provided. They will discuss how they differ and write their own opening.

Pupil practice

Get started

Children read the two extracts and discuss the questions with a partner before writing their answer.

Suggested answers

1. The first story opens with dialogue (beginning with a question) and then introduces a character and their funny thoughts.
The second story opens with a description of a character and invites the reader to ask: What happened to change Kitty's mind about being small?
Children should make any or all of these observations. [2 marks]

2. Children give their opinions of the extracts. [1 mark]

3. The main aim of a story opening is to make the reader want to read more. [1 mark]

Try these

Children write different opening sentences using the different techniques specified.

Suggested answers

1. *"How did you two get so dirty?" asked Jake's mother.* [example]

2. Accept a sentence that describes a character. [1 mark]

3. Accept a sentence that describes a setting. [1 mark]

4. Accept a sentence that describes some action. [1 mark]

5. Accept a sentence that asks a question. [1 mark]

6. Accept a sentence that tells the reader something interesting. [1 mark]

Now try these

Children use a sentence from their answers in **Try these** and plan the rest of their story opening. They are reminded that the opening must attract the reader's attention.

Suggested answers

1. Accept plans/ideas that show understanding of the different ways of opening a story and that attempt to grab the reader's attention. Reward creativity and good ideas.

2. Accept story openings that show understanding of the different ways of doing this and that attempt to achieve the aim of grabbing the reader's attention. Reward creativity, good ideas and good language skills.

You may wish to use the activities and photocopiables in **Support and Embed** to give differentiated support with these activities.

Support, embed & challenge

Support

Ensure the children understand the difference between the opening techniques outlined by using different techniques to start the same story. Support the children as they complete Unit 4 Resource 1: Story openings – sentences, which is a template for a shortened version of the activity in **Try these**. When they have finished, ask them to choose their favourite sentence and use it to create a longer, more detailed verbal story opening.

Embed

Ask these children to choose their favourite story opener from **Try these**, or a new opener if they prefer, and use it to plan the first paragraph of a story (**Now try these** question 1). When they are ready, Unit 4 Resource 2: Story openings – paragraph provides a template for **Now try these** question 2. The children write their opening, plan the rest of the story and write the second paragraph. They can then plan the rest of their story and write the next paragraph.

Challenge

Ask the children to continue and finish the story from the extract by Bel Mooney – 'It's not fair … that I'm little'.

Homework / Additional activities

Story openings

Ask the children to look in storybooks at home and make a list of the different ways that these stories open. They should be prepared to bring their list to school and to share their findings with the class. They could also look at how stories told in film or on TV open and make a list of these.

Collins Connect: Unit 4

Ask the children to complete Unit 4 (see Teach → Year 3 → Composition → Unit 4).

Unit 5: Characters in stories

Overview

English curriculum objectives

Year 3 Children should be taught to plan their writing by:

- discussing writing similar to that which they are planning to write
- organising paragraphs around a theme
- in narratives, creating settings, characters and plot.

Building towards

Children will plan and write their own story based around a character.

Treasure House resources

- Composition Skills Pupil Book 3, Unit 5, pages 16–18
- Collins Connect Treasure House Composition Year 3, Unit 5
- Photocopiable Unit 5, Resource 1: My character, page 72
- Photocopiable Unit 5, Resource 2: Planning my character's story, page 73

Additional resources

- Narratives where there are strong characters.
- Extracts of character descriptions

Introduction

Teaching overview

This unit focuses on developing children's understanding of how to identify and describe characters in narrative settings. It stresses the point that there are different ways to show the reader a character and looks at how an author might describe a character's thoughts, feelings and actions as well as what they look like. Children read an extract from the fable 'The Tortoise and the Hare' and analyse the character descriptions. They finally plan a character of their own and write a story based around that character.

'The Tortoise and the Hare' is probably the best known of the fables told by the ancient Greek writer Aesop, who lived in the 6th Century BCE. The fable is a perfect example of the art of storytelling, with a clear structure and development and two contrasting characters in conflict.

Introduce the concept

Remind children of the class story they are reading at present. Ask them to discuss with a partner the characters in that book. They should summarise the characters and evaluate how they feel about them. Ask: 'How has the author described the characters?' Take feedback.

Ask children what techniques the author uses to make the characters seem alive for the reader. There are broadly four ways:

1. By describing them to us directly

2. By showing us how a character acts

3. By showing us what a character says or thinks

4. By showing us what a character feels

Explain that they are going to read an extract from one of *Aesop's Fables* with two very different characters. As they read the extract, they should consider how the author has portrayed each character and the techniques he has used to achieve this.

Pupil practice

Get started

Children discuss the questions about the characters with a partner and feed back to the class.

Suggested answers

1. Children give their opinion of Hare. Better answers will draw on evidence in the text. [1 mark]
2. Children look for evidence in the text for their opinion of Hare. [1 mark]
3. Children give their opinion of Tortoise. Better answers will draw on evidence in the text. [1 mark]
4. Children look for evidence in the text for their opinion of Tortoise. [1 mark]

Try these

Children invent a character of their own and answer questions about their character.

Suggested answers

1. Accept answers that provide a character choice. [1 mark]
2. Accept answers that provide a character's name. [1 mark]
3. Accept answers that give an adjective to describe their character. [1 mark]

4. Accept answers that give the character's thoughts. [1 mark]
5. Accept answers that give the character's actions. [1 mark]
6. Accept answers that give a line of speech the character might say. [1 mark]

Now try these

The children write a description of and a story about the character they created in **Try these**.

1. Accept a description of the character from children's previous planning. Descriptions should be in full sentences and correctly punctuated. Reward creativity, descriptive prowess and generally good writing and language skills.
2. Accept a short story about the character invented previously. There should be examples of vivid description and attempts to show the character in other ways through what they think, feel, say and do. Reward creativity and generally good writing and language skills.

You may wish to use the activities and photocopiables in **Support and Embed** to give differentiated support with these activities.

Support, embed & challenge

Support

Unit 5 Resource 1: My character provides support for the children as they complete a simplified version of **Try these**. Afterwards, ask the children to describe their character to a partner and tell a short anecdote about their character.

Embed

Once the children have completed **Now try these** question 1, ask them to use Unit 5 Resource 2: Planning my character's story to plan the story that they will write in **Now try these** question 2.

Challenge

Ask these children to use the planning for their character's story to write the full narrative. They should consider the different ways to reveal character and make the character come alive for the reader.

Homework / Additional activities

What are the characters like?

Ask the children to look at a range of storybooks at home and to talk about the characters in these stories to someone at home. They draw one or two of the characters and show these to the class. The other children could then comment on the drawings, saying what they think the drawing says about the character. You could introduce this activity by showing children illustrations of famous storybook characters.

Collins Connect: Unit 5

Ask the children to complete Unit 5 (see Teach → Year 3 → Composition → Unit 5).

Unit 6: Continuing a story

Overview

English curriculum objectives

Year 3 Children should be taught to plan their writing by:

- discussing writing similar to that which they are planning to write
- organising paragraphs around a theme
- in narratives, creating settings, characters and plot.

Treasure House resources

- Composition Skills Pupil Book 3, Unit 6, pages 19–21
- Collins Connect Treasure House Composition Year 3, Unit 6

- Photocopiable Unit 6, Resource 1: Continuing a story: King Arthur, page 74
- Photocopiable Unit 6, Resource 2: Continuing a story: Merlin, page 75

Additional resources

- Modern retellings of the story of King Arthur and his knights for children to browse and read

Introduction

Teaching overview

This unit focuses on developing children's understanding of the features of a longer story and how to keep the reader's interest. The unit provides an extract from the beginning of a story about the legendary British king Arthur where the reader is introduced to the setting and the main characters. The plot is also introduced, but not developed.

Children are encouraged to analyse the text, asking questions as they read about what might happen next using the clues in the extract. They then consider how the story might continue and what might happen to the characters.

The story of King Arthur and his knights is a common subject in medieval English and French literature, appearing notably in the sprawling compendium of tales *Le Morte d'Arthur* (1485) by Thomas Malory (c.1415–71).

Introduce the concept

Remind children of the previous work on character and setting and how often a story is woven around a problem that needs solving (see Unit 1). Tell them that they will read an extract from the beginning of a story about a famous king from legend called Arthur. Ask the children to share anything they already know about King Arthur and the Knights of the Round Table. Tell them they are about to the read the beginning of a very long story about Arthur.

Share the extract in class, having asked the children to think about how an author makes his readers curious about how the narrative will unfold and so keep reading.

Once the children have completed the tasks, allow them time to browse the retellings of the legend of King Arthur that you have sourced.

Pupil practice

Pupil Book pages 19–21

Get started

Children discuss the questions about the story with a partner and feed back to the class.

Suggested answers

1. Children discuss what information on the story of King Arthur is included in the extract.

2. Questions may include: Who is Merlin? What was Arthur in danger from when he was a baby? Is Arthur still in danger now? How did Arthur's father die? Is Arthur's mother still alive? Will all the other knights be happy that Arthur is king? Will Arthur be a good king? Does Arthur even want to be king?

3. Children can choose any character (Merlin is the most likely choice) and should discuss why they find them mysterious.

Try these

Children answer questions about Arthur.

Suggested answers

1. Accept answers that speculate about the threat to Arthur as a baby. [1 mark]

2. Accept answers that speculate about threats faced by Arthur in the present story. [1 mark]

3. Accept answers that speculate about how Arthur's father died. [1 mark]

4. Accept answers that speculate about his mother. [1 mark]

5. Accept answers that speculate about the other knights. [1 mark]

6. Accept answers for any speculation about Arthur's ability as, and willingness to be, king. [1 mark]

Now try these

Children write the next part of the story, using their answers from **Try these** to prompt it.

Suggested answers

1. Accept a continuation of the story where there are evident attempts to build on the extract and show what happens next. Reward creativity, good writing and language skills, as well as good use of the children's ideas from the previous section.

2. Accept attempts at the next episode where the focus is on Merlin: his character, his history and/ or what he does next. Accept evident attempts to build on the story so far. Reward creativity, and good writing and language skills.

You may wish to use the activities and photocopiables in **Support and Embed** to give differentiated support with these activities.

Support, embed & challenge

Support

Ask these children to concentrate on **Now try these** activity 1. the children to invent the next part of the story. They should consider their answers to the questions in **Try these** to help them plan their story and then use the storyboard to shape their ideas. Unit 6 Resource 1: Continuing a story: King Arthur supports this.

Embed

Once the children have written the second part of the story (**Now try these** question 1), provide them with Unit 6 Resource 2: Continuing a story: Merlin on which to write **Now try these** question 2. Here, the children write the third section of the story: Merlin has heard about Arthur. What will happen next? Remind them of the notes and questions they wrote in **Get started** and **Try these**.

Challenge

These children should consider the knights' response to the crowning of Arthur as king. Ask them to write a new episode from the point of view of one of the knights who is not happy with Arthur as King of England.

Homework / Additional activities

King Arthur

Ask the children to research the story of how King Arthur was eventually killed in battle and what happened to his famous sword. They should write a summary of it ready to read to the class. They could draw a picture to accompany the summary.

Collins Connect: Unit 6

Ask the children to complete Unit 6 (see Teach → Year 3 → Composition → Unit 6).

Unit 7: Paragraphs in stories

Overview

English curriculum objectives

Year 3 children should be taught to draft and write by:

- composing and rehearsing sentences orally (including dialogue)
- organising paragraphs around a theme
- in narratives, creating settings, characters and plot.

Building towards

Children will write their own paragraph, showing an understanding of why writers use paragraphs.

Treasure House resources

- Composition Skills Pupil Book 3, Unit 7, pages 22–24
- Collins Connect Treasure House Composition Year 3, Unit 7
- Photocopiable Unit 7, Resource 1: My new paragraph, page 76
- Photocopiable Unit 7, Resource 2: Paragraph checklist, page 77

Additional resources

- A collection of storybooks with good use of paragraphing for children to browse and read

Introduction

Teaching overview

This unit focuses on the use of paragraphs in fiction and uses a story showing clear, effective use of paragraphing. Writing needs to be organised into paragraphs to make the text readable and the narrative easy to understand. Each paragraph in the extract shows a reason why the author decided to start a new 'chunk' of text. Children are invited to read the text and to consider how the paragraphs have been used to organise the composition.

Introduce the concept

Ask children to share with a partner what they already know about the use of paragraphs in stories. Take feedback and have a whole class discussion with reference to a class story you are reading. Show examples from this book and others. You might like to show the children what a story would look like if it were written without paragraphs – would they want to read it at all? Tell them, though, that there is another good reason to write in paragraphs – to organise the story.

Tell children that they will read a short story that is organised into paragraphs. They will analyse the text and discuss why and when a new paragraph is needed. They will add a new paragraph to the ending of the story giving a clear reason as to why the shift was needed. They will write rules for changing paragraphs.

Pupil practice

Get started

Children read the extract and then answer general questions about the use of paragraphs.

Answers

1. Paragraphs should be used to organise writing and to break it into easier-to-read sections.
2. You should start a new paragraph if the story moves to a different time or place; if a new character starts to speak; or for dramatic effect.

Try these

Children read the story and answer questions about it. The questions refer to paragraphs.

Answers

1. Shadow and Tom   [1 mark]
2. A Christmas in the past   [1 mark]
3. For dramatic effect   [1 mark]
4. In the kitchen   [1 mark]
5. Outside   [1 mark]
6. Speech/dialogue   [1 mark]
7. The phrase 'That was many years ago now'.   [1 mark]

Now try these

Children are asked to add one more paragraph that continues the story then to write a set of rules about writing paragraphs.

1. Paragraphs must either move the story to a different time or place or begin with dialogue. Children may choose to introduce a new character. There should be clear attempts to build on the story so far and show what happens next. Reward creativity and good writing and language skills.
2. Children are asked to explain in their own words when to start a new paragraph.

   Paragraph rules must include the following recommendations, written in the child's own words. Children may include examples.

   When writing fiction, you should start a new paragraph:

   • if the story moves to a different time or place
   • if a new character starts to speak
   • for dramatic effect.

You may wish to use the activities and photocopiables in **Support and Embed** to give differentiated support with these activities.

Support, embed & challenge

Support

Ask the children to use the prompts provided in Unit 7 Resource 1: My new paragraph to write an additional paragraph to add to the end of 'Shadow'. (**Now try these** question 1). Next, ask them to work with a partner to remember the key reasons for starting a new paragraph.

Embed

When the children have added their extra paragraphs to the story (**Now try these** question 1) ask them to use Unit 7 Resource 2: Paragraph checklist to write their own explanations to a new class of Year 3 children about the use of paragraphs in fiction. They can give examples from 'Shadow'.

Challenge

Ask the children to write the prequel to the story 'Shadow'. How did the dog get to be so bony and dirty? Where had it been? They should remember to use paragraphs to organise the material.

Homework / Additional activities

Paragraph shifts

Ask children to find examples of paragraph shifts in their storybooks at home. They should use one or two books and make a list of the reasons why the author moved to a new paragraph.

Collins Connect: Unit 7

Ask the children to complete Unit 7 (see Teach → Year 3 → Composition → Unit 7).

Review unit 1

These tasks provide the children with the opportunity to apply and demonstrate the skills they have learned.

Explain to the children that they now have an opportunity to show their skills independently. Read through the task with the children and make sure they have understood what to do.

A. Story settings

Look for evidence of children's developing understanding of and writing of a descriptive paragraph. Significant features to look out for include:

- noun phrases
- sensory information – what could be seen, heard, smelt, and so on
- descriptions of the details in the scene.

B. Characters in stories

Look for evidence of children's developing understanding of how to write a character description. Significant features to look out for include:

- a description of the character's thoughts, feelings and actions
- a description of what they look like.

C. Using dialogue

Look for evidence of children's developing understanding of how to punctuate speech correctly. Significant features to look out for include:

- putting speech marks at the start and end of spoken words
- putting a capital letter at the start of the speech
- punctuating the speech before closing speech marks.

Answers

- "You are one of the most ridiculous-looking people I have ever seen," <u>said</u> the bow tie.
- "You look ridiculous!" <u>shouted</u> Mrs Baxter.
- "I beg your pardon," <u>said</u> Mr Baxter.
- "Mary!" <u>cried</u> Mr Baxter, running out of the bathroom.
- "Mary, this bow tie just spoke to me," I <u>exclaimed</u>.

Unit 8: Writing a rhyming poem (1)

Overview

English curriculum objectives

Reading: Year 3 children should be taught to develop positive attitudes to reading and understanding of what they read by:

- listening to and discussing a wide range of fiction and poetry
- preparing poems and play scripts to read aloud and to perform, showing understanding through intonation, tone, volume and action
- recognising some different forms of poetry (for example free verse, narrative poetry).

Writing: Year 3 children should be taught to plan their writing by discussing writing similar to that which they are planning to write in order to understand and learn from its structure.

Building towards

Children will write a short rhyming poem.

Treasure House resources

- Composition Skills Pupil Book 3, Unit 8, pages 27–29
- Collins Connect Treasure House Composition Year 3, Unit 8
- Photocopiable Unit 8, Resource 1: My rhyming poem, page 78
- Photocopiable Unit 8, Resource 2: My season poem, page 79

Additional resources

- A selection of rhyming poems for children to browse and read
- A children's rhyming dictionary (book or online site)

Introduction

Teaching overview

This unit focuses on the use of rhyme in poetry. Not all poems rhyme but some do. Rhyming words are words that sound the same. A rhyme scheme is the pattern of rhyming words at the ends of the lines. Children read the poem 'Water' by the British poet John R. Crossland and analyse its rhyme scheme. They practise rhyming and move on to write their own four-line poem. When they have written their poems, it is suggested that the class holds a poetry performance where the children recite and preform their poems.

Introduce the concept

Share a short rhyming poem with the class and ask children whether they notice anything special about it: it rhymes. Check children's understanding of the meaning of rhyme and ask for examples.

Show the same poem on an interactive whiteboard or similar and read through it again, discussing with the children which words rhyme. Ask: 'Do you notice anything about the pattern the rhymes make?' This is called the rhyme scheme.

Explain that they will be reading a short poem, analysing the rhyme scheme and writing their own poems.

Pupil practice

Pupil Book pages 27–29

Get started

Children read the poem then discuss the questions about rhyme with a partner. They make a list of rhyming words in the poem.

Answers

1. Rhyming words are words that sound the same. [1 mark]
2. A rhyme scheme is the pattern of rhyming words in a poem. [1 mark]
3. Six rhyming pairs: all/waterfall; smell/well; about/out; rain/again; eyes/try; tears/ears [6 marks]

Try these

Children copy and complete the table, adding rhyming words to those given. Accept any correctly rhyming words for each group, awarding a mark for each.

Now try these

1. Children write a four-line poem using the same rhyming pattern as the given poem.
2. The children analyse the rhyme scheme of a poem then write their own six-line rhyming poem about their favourite season.

Suggested answers

1. Accept a four-line poem on the prescribed subject of snow or sun. Lines 1 and 3 and lines 2 and 4 must rhyme. Reward creativity and good writing and language skills, especially any use of poetic language or techniques.
2. The rhyme scheme is aabb... Accept a poem six lines long on the subject of the child's favourite season and using the same rhyme scheme. Reward creativity and good writing and language skills, especially any use of poetic language or techniques.

You may wish to use the activities and photocopiables in **Support and Embed** to give differentiated support with these activities.

Support, embed & challenge

Support

These children can use Unit 8 Resource 1: My rhyming poem to support them in the **Now try these** activity as they write a four-line poem called 'Snow' or 'The Sun'. They need to rhyme lines 1/3 and 2/4.

Embed

Once the children have written their first poem, ask them to carry out **Now try these** question 2. Challenge them to work out the rhyming scheme for

the poem (aabb) then use a similar pattern for their own poem. Unit 8 Resource 2: My season poem provides a template for the children to use for their poem.

Challenge

These children can write their own rhyming poem, using a rhyme scheme of their choice. They can choose the subject matter or it can be drawn from across the curriculum.

Homework / Additional activities

Finding rhymes

Ask the children to find as many rhyming word pairs at home as they can (for example, door/floor). They should make a list and bring it to school to share.

Collins Connect: Unit 8

Ask the children to complete Unit 8 (see Teach → Year 3 → Composition → Unit 8).

Unit 9: Writing a non-rhyming poem

Overview

English curriculum objectives

Reading: Year 3 children should be taught to develop positive attitudes to reading and understanding of what they read by:

- listening to and discussing a wide range of fiction and poetry
- preparing poems and play scripts to read aloud and to perform, showing understanding through intonation, tone, volume and action
- recognising some different forms of poetry (for example free verse, narrative poetry).

Writing: Year 3 children should be taught to plan their writing by discussing writing similar to that which they are planning to write in order to understand and learn from its structure.

Building towards

Children will write a short non-rhyming poem.

Treasure House resources

- Composition Skills Pupil Book 3, Unit 9, pages 30–32
- Collins Connect Treasure House Composition Year 3, Unit 9
- Photocopiable Unit 9, Resource 1: My descriptive phrases, page 80
- Photocopiable Unit 9, Resource 2: From my window, page 81

Additional resources

- A selection of non-rhyming poems for children to browse and read

Introduction

Teaching overview

This unit focuses on non-rhyming poetry. Many poems rhyme, but not all do. Some poets use different techniques in their poetry other than rhyme. These include:

- rhythm (the beat created by the words)
- personification (human qualities given to inanimate objects)
- powerful descriptive language (striking nouns, verbs and adjectives)
- alliteration (repeated use of the same sound)
- onomatopoeia (a word that sounds like the thing it is naming)
- metaphor and simile.

Children read the poem 'From My Window' by Chris Whitney and analyse its structure and the poetic techniques used. They practise writing short descriptive phrases before writing a poem based on the structure of the poem in the unit. When they have written their poems, it is suggested that the class holds a poetry performance where the children recite their poems.

Introduce the concept

Remind children of the rhyming poems they looked at in Unit 8 and ask them whether they think all poems should rhyme and if they know any poems that don't. Ask them to come up with other techniques that can make a poem a poem, take feedback and record their ideas as a spider diagram (see Teaching overview above).

Explain that they will be reading a short poem, analysing the techniques used and then writing their own poems.

Pupil practice

Get started

Ask the children to read the poem then discuss the questions about the poem with a partner.

Answers

1. The poet sees daffodils, bluebells, crocuses and primroses in a street. **[4 marks]**

2. The poet sees sheep and lambs on a hill and crows flying to and from their nests in trees. **[2 marks]**

3. The poet sees new buds opening on the branches of trees. **[1 mark]**

Try these

Children copy and complete the table, adding words under the headings of Alliteration, Onomatopoeia, Adjectives.

Answers

1. **Alliteration:** petals painting, crows caw-caw, bare branches, buds burst **[1 mark for each example]**

2. **Onomatopoeia:** caw-caw **[1 mark]**

3. **Adjectives:** yellow, blue, big, tallest, bare, new **[1 mark for each example]**

Now try these

Children write short phrases describing what they might see from a window in winter. They then use these phrases to write a non-rhyming poem called 'From My Window' using the descriptive phrases.

Answers

1. Accept phrases describing what they might see from a window in winter. Look for quality descriptive phrases. Reward the use of adjectives, alliteration and any other poetic devices.

2. Children write a non-rhyming poem about looking through or out of a window in winter. Reward the use of adjectives and any other poetic devices such as alliteration, onomatopoeia, personification and repetition for effect.

You may wish to use the activities and photocopiables in **Support and Embed** to give differentiated support with these activities.

Support, embed & challenge

Support

Unit 9 Resource 1: My descriptive phrases provides a simplified version of the activities in **Now try these**. The children are asked to draw three scenes and describe them. Help the children use their descriptions to write a simple non-rhyming verse.

Embed

Once the children have noted a range of descriptive phrases (**Now try these**) ask them to use Unit 9 Resource 2: From my window to write their poem.

Once they have finished, ask them to swap poems with a partner. Ask the children to read each other's poems and make comments about the poetic techniques covered.

Challenge

Ask the children to write their own non-rhyming poem. It should be based on someone who is outside in winter looking in through a window at a warm cosy room. Ask them to call it 'Looking in Through the Window'. They may choose to use the same format employed by the poem in the unit.

Homework / Additional activities

What's through your window?

Ask the children to write a list of things they can see through a window in their home. Ask them to bring their lists to school and the class can write a collaborative non-rhyming poem using the lists.

Collins Connect: Unit 9

Ask the children to complete Unit 9 (see Teach → Year 3 → Composition → Unit 9).

# Unit 10: Planning non-fiction

Overview

English curriculum objectives

Year 3 Children should be taught to plan their writing by:

- discussing writing similar to that which they are planning to write in order to understand and learn from its structure.

Year 3 children should be taught to draft and write by:

- organising paragraphs around a theme
- in non-narrative material, using simple organisational devices (for example headings and subheadings).

Building towards

Children will plan and write a short non-chronological report.

Treasure House resources

- Composition Skills Pupil Book 3, Unit 10, pages 33–35
- Collins Connect Treasure House Composition Year 3, Unit 10
- Photocopiable Unit 10, Resource 1: Planning my report, page 82
- Photocopiable Unit 10, Resource 2: My report, page 83

Additional resources

- A selection of non-fiction books about animals, wildlife, and so on for children to browse and read
- Non-fiction film clip about sharks
- Website about sharks

Introduction

Teaching overview

This unit focuses on planning a unit of non-fiction writing – a non-chronological report. It concentrates on the structure of the report – in particular the use of paragraphs, headings, subheadings and bullet points. It stresses that this type of report provides facts and therefore needs organising carefully in order to give clear information to the reader. Children should be aware of the need to consider their audience and that this will inform their planning of the text. Children will consider how to plan a non-chronological text, building up to the writing of a short report.

Introduce the concept

Watch a short film clip about sharks and ask children to discuss what information has been provided.

Ask: 'How could the information be categorised? Was it information about habitat or feeding habits? Was it about the species or the lifecycle?' Stress that in both documentary films and books information needs to be organised or grouped together to make understanding easier for the viewer or reader.

Using an interactive whiteboard, look at a website about sharks and discuss with children how the information has been organised. You could record children's ideas in a structured table like the one in the unit.

Tell children that they are learning about organising information into a report. Ask them to share what they already know about writing information texts.

Pupil practice

Get started

The children read the introduction and text then answer questions with a partner about planning non-fiction.

Answers

1. It is important to plan non-fiction writing because the information in the text needs to be organised so that the reader can understand it easily. [1 mark]
2. The first thing to decide is the purpose of the text, as this will determine the type of non-fiction text you will write. [1 mark]
3. The purpose of this non-fiction text is to inform the reader about sharks. [1 mark]

Try these

Children answer questions about the report on sharks.

Answers

1. The report includes information on what sharks are, what they eat and how they reproduce. [1 mark]
2. The information is grouped into paragraphs and organised with headings, subheadings and bullet points. [1 mark]

3. The subheading for each section tells the reader what the section is about. [1 mark]
4. A conclusion should sum up the report. [1 mark]
5. Accept answers that show understanding of the purpose of a conclusion and its relevance to the content of the report. [up to 3 marks]

Now try these

Children complete a table providing information as to what they would include in the different sections of a report on a creature of their choice. They consider the titles used in the subheadings. They then write a short report on their chosen creature.

Answers

1. Reward understanding that the information needs to be grouped and that each section needs an appropriate subheading.
2. Reward good organisation of information and use of organisational devices, such as paragraphs, subheadings and bullet-point lists. Reports should include an introduction and a conclusion and, if children wish, illustrations and diagrams.

You may wish to use the activities and photocopiables in **Support and Embed** to give differentiated support with these activities.

Support, embed & challenge

Support

Use Unit 10 Resource 1: Planning my report with those children who would benefit from a simpler planning sheet for **Now try these**. Once the children have completed their report, help them to transfer their notes into a simple report, using a sentence-length paragraph for each element of their spider diagram.

Embed

Once the children have completed their planning, provide them with Unit 10 Resource 2: My report on which to write their report. The resource sheet reminds the children to add an introduction and a conclusion.

Challenge

Ask these children to write a non-chronological report on a subject of their choice – possibly a hobby or interest.

Homework / Additional activities

My family report

Ask the children to write a non-chronological report about their family. What would be in the different sections? What could the subheadings be?

Collins Connect: Unit 10

Ask the children to complete Unit 10 (see Teach → Year 3 → Composition → Unit 10).

Unit 11: Writing an information text (1)

Overview

English curriculum objectives

Children should be taught to plan their writing by:

- discussing writing similar to that which they are planning to write in order to understand and learn from its structure

Children should be taught to draft and write by:

- organising paragraphs around a theme
- in non-narrative material, using simple organisational devices (for example headings and subheadings).

Building towards

Children will write a short information report.

Treasure House resources

- Composition Skills Pupil Book 3, Unit 11, pages 36–38
- Collins Connect Treasure House Composition Year 3, Unit 11
- Photocopiable Unit 11 Resource 1: Planning my report, page 84
- Photocopiable Unit 11 Resource 2: My report, page 85

Additional resources

- A selection of non-fiction books or articles about ICT for children to browse and read

Introduction

Teaching overview

This unit focuses on writing an information text and consolidates and builds on work in the previous unit. It concentrates on one method of organising information, looking at the aim of the text, how the information has been organised, the language used and the use of a bullet-pointed list. There are clearly organised sections, headings and subheadings. Children should be aware of the need to consider their audience. They decide on a topic that interests them, plan a report about it and then write the report. The text used here is about communication technologies (sending messages) and, where possible, this unit can be taught in conjunction with an objective from the Year 3 ICT curriculum. You may wish to suggest that they write about an ICT-related topic or a type of technology.

Introduce the concept

You might like to start the lesson by reading together an ICT-related information text other than that used in the unit. Ask the children to comment on its structure and organisation and to share what they already know about the main features of information texts. These include:

- use of headings and subheadings
- use of a clear structure of introduction, main body and conclusion
- clear use of paragraphs
- technical vocabulary
- formal language
- occasional use of bullet-point lists.

Pupil practice

Get started

Children read the text and answer questions with a partner about non-fiction reports.

Answers

1. The purpose of a non-fiction report is to inform the reader about something.
2. This report aims to inform the reader about sending messages in the past and present.

Try these

Children answer questions about the information text.

Answers

1. The information has been organised into sections according to topic. [1 mark]
2. The first section, 'Sending messages', is an introduction. [1 mark]
3. The second section provides information on mobile phones. [1 mark]
4. The third section provides information on computers and the internet. [1 mark]

5. The author uses a bullet-point list because it is the clearest way to present the information. [1 mark]
6. Answers may include: text message internet, information, computers, wire, online. [1 mark for each example]

Now try these

Children think of a topic that interests them and answer questions relating to it. You may want to suggest they write about an ICT-related topic or a type of technology. They then write the information text.

Answers

1. Children should answer each question with details of what they will include in a report on the subject.
2. Reports should include an introduction and a conclusion, use of subheadings and a bullet-point list. Reward use of paragraphs, good structure and organisation of information and any additional organisational devices.

You may wish to use the activities and photocopiables in **Support and Embed** to give differentiated support with these activities.

Support, embed & challenge

Support

Once the children have answered the questions in **Now try these** question 1, provide children who require support with question 2 with Unit 11 Resource 1: Planning my report. This provides a structure for the report and will support children as they create a text with paragraphs and subheadings, to help them organise the information.

Embed

Once the children have answered the questions in **Now try these** question 1, provide the children with

Unit 11 Resource 2: My report on which to write their report. Ask them to use the checklist to help them remember the features they need to include.

Challenge

Ask these children to write an information text related to another class topic. The subject may be drawn from across the curriculum. They should write independently, without the need for structured support.

Homework / Additional activities

The World Wide Web

Ask the children to research information about the development of the World Wide Web and plan a short information report about it. What sections should they include? What information would readers want to know? If they have time they could write the report and include illustrations.

Collins Connect: Unit 11

Ask the children to complete Unit 11 (see Teach → Year 3 → Composition → Unit 11).

Unit 12: Writing instructions

Overview

English curriculum objectives

Year 3 Children should be taught to plan their writing by:

- discussing writing similar to that which they are planning to write in order to understand and learn from its structure.

Year 3 children should be taught to draft and write by:

- in non-narrative material, using simple organisational devices (for example headings and subheadings).

Building towards

Children will plan and write instructions for a recipe.

Treasure House resources

- Composition Skills Pupil Book 3, Unit 12, pages 39–41
- Collins Connect Treasure House Composition Year 3, Unit 12
- Photocopiable Unit 12, Resource 1: Getting ready to cook, page 86
- Photocopiable Unit 12, Resource 2: My recipe, page 87

Additional resources

- Some board games (such as Ludo and Snakes and Ladders) with simple instructions
- A selection of books and leaflets containing instructions for children to browse and read. Include some recipe books.

Introduction

Teaching overview

This unit focuses on writing instructions: texts that tell the reader how to do something. There are many different types of instructions, such as directions, recipes, how to assemble furniture, what to do if there is a fire in a building, and so on. Because instructions tell the reader what to do they contain imperative verbs – which children may know as command (or 'bossy') verbs – and often take the form of a numbered sequential list. Time adverbials, such as 'first', 'next', 'finally', and so on are another possibility.

Introduce the concept

Organise the class so that there is a board game on each table along with a set of instructions. Games like Snakes and Ladders, Ludo or Boggle would be ideal. Ask children to read the instructions

and to have a go at playing the game. Stop after a few minutes and ask the class to discuss how the sets of instructions worked. Ask: 'What features were the same for each set of instructions?' Children may suggest the following:

- object of the game
- equipment needed to play the game
- a numbered list showing how to play the game.

Elicit what children already know about writing instructions. Tell them that this unit builds on their prior knowledge.

Ask: 'What type of verbs do we usually find in a set of instructions?' Agree that we usually find imperative (command) verbs and that they will need to use these in the recipes they will be writing later. Explain that game instructions are often written without imperatives.

Pupil practice

Get started

Children answer questions with a partner.

Suggested answers

1. Children discuss instructions they have followed in the past.
2. Children discuss what the instructions were for.
3. Children make a list of examples of written instructions. These may include directions, recipes, how to put furniture together, or what to do if there is a fire.

Try these

Children answer questions about the text provided – Snakes and Ladders.

Answers

1. These instructions explain how to play the game Snakes and Ladders. [1 mark]
2. The information has been organised into sections with subheadings. [1 mark]
3. The instructions are written in the order in which they should be carried out. [1 mark]
4. You could order instructions by using time adverbials, such as 'first', 'next' and 'finally'. [1 mark]

5. Imperative verbs should be used. [1 mark]
6. Children write a list of imperative verbs.
[1 mark for each correct verb]

Now try these

1. The children choose what type of sandwich they would like to make and list ingredients and equipment.
2. The children write a recipe for their chosen sandwich.

Suggested answers

1. Children make a list of the equipment and ingredients they will need in order to make a sandwich.
2. Accept an organised set of instructions, correctly ordered and using numbers and/or adverbials and imperative (command) verbs. Reward clear, methodical instructions and check that all steps in the process are present.

You may wish to use the activities and photocopiables in **Support and Embed** to give differentiated support with these activities.

Support, embed & challenge

Support

Ask the children who need support with **Now try these** question 1 to complete the planning sheet (see Unit 12 Resource 1: Getting ready to cook). It supports them as they consider what equipment and ingredients will be needed to make their chosen sandwich.

Embed

Once the children have completed the ingredients and equipment list for their chosen sandwich (**Now try these** question 1), ask them to write the 'What to do' list of instructions on Unit 12 Resource 2: My recipe. Remind them to draw a diagram to accompany each point and to use imperative verbs.

Challenge

Ask these children to write a set of instructions for making a two-course meal – main course and dessert – of their choice. They could take inspiration from their school dinners and could even talk to the cook! They will need to research the recipes for ingredients and method prior to writing, but the finished instructions should be in their own words.

Homework / Additional activities

Instructions for making a meal

Ask the children to watch a meal being prepared at home and to make a list of the equipment and ingredients. They should watch carefully as the food is prepared – they may even video it – and write the set of instructions to accompany this.

Collins Connect: Unit 12

Ask the children to complete Unit 12 (see Teach → Year 3 → Composition → Unit 12).

Unit 13: Paragraphs in non-fiction

Overview

English curriculum objectives

Year 3 Children should be taught to plan their writing by:

- discussing writing similar to that which they are planning to write in order to understand and learn from its structure.

Year 3 children should be taught to draft and write by:

- organising paragraphs around a theme
- in non-narrative material, using simple organisational devices (for example, headings and subheadings).

Building towards

Children will plan and write a report making clear use of paragraphs.

Treasure House resources

- Composition Skills Pupil Book 3, Unit 13, pages 42–44
- Collins Connect Treasure House Composition Year 3, Unit 13
- Photocopiable Unit 13, Resource 1: My topic sentences, page 88
- Photocopiable Unit 13, Resource 2: My paragraphs, page 89

Additional resources

- A selection of non-fiction books, including some about rivers, for children to browse and read
- A photocopied short non-fiction text cut up into paragraphs, one set for each table or group. Make sure that each paragraph has a distinct topic/theme and, if possible, uses a clear topic sentence.

Introduction

Teaching overview

This unit focuses on the use of paragraphs in non-fiction writing and relates to work on the use of paragraphs in fiction carried out in Unit 7. A paragraph is a group of sentences that have one theme in common. Most paragraphs have two or more sentences in them, but some only have one. It is hard to read a big block of writing, so paragraphs break up the text into easy-to-read sections. In printed books, new paragraphs are sometimes indented or separated from the preceding paragraph by a little extra space. In their own writing, children should be encouraged to use an indent to show a new paragraph.

The extract about rivers makes clear use of paragraphs to organise the information. Children read this extract and examine how it has been organised. They note the internal structure of a paragraph – each introduced by a topic sentence – and how they build to form the whole piece of writing. A topic sentence tells the reader what the paragraph is going to be about.

Introduce the concept

Ask children to share with a partner what they know already about the use of paragraphs in fiction. Take feedback from the class and explain that paragraphs are also used in organising information in non-fiction.

Provide groups of children with a set of cut-up paragraphs and ask them to put them in order (they could number them). Ask the children to be prepared to justify why they have put them in that order. Use this activity to talk about the role of paragraphs, including topic sentences, and how paragraphs are often presented in both printed and handwritten texts (using an indent).

Pupil practice

Pupil book pages 42–44

Get started

Children read the text and discuss the answers to these questions with a partner before writing.

Answers

1. A paragraph is a sentence or group of sentences that have one theme in common.

2. Paragraphs break up the text into easy-to-read sections and help to organise the order of information.

3. This text has five paragraphs.

4. Each new paragraph starts on a new line and should be indented.

Try these

Children answer questions about the topic sentence in each paragraph.

Answers

Paragraph 1: Rivers have ages just like we do – a river can be 'young', 'middle aged' or 'old'.   [1 mark]

Paragraph 2: The first or 'young' age is when the river begins, high up in the hills or mountains.

[1 mark]

Paragraph 3: When a river is 'middle aged', it has reached flatter land and is not rushing down steep slopes   [1 mark]

Paragraph 4: An 'old' river is the part of the river near the sea.   [1 mark]

Paragraph 5: There are some very famous rivers in the world.   [1 mark]

Now try these

Children plan five paragraphs about their favourite sport or interest. They add the topic sentences to all five and move on to write additional sentences within each paragraph.

Suggested answers

1. Accept five planned paragraphs on a chosen sport, interest, hobby or pastime. Planning must include topic sentences.

2. Children must include additional information under the topic sentence.

You may wish to use the activities and photocopiables in **Support and Embed** to give differentiated support with these activities.

Support, embed & challenge

Support

Once the children have written their notes for **Now try these** question 1, ask them to complete Unit 13 Resource 1: My topic sentences which provides a simple template on which to write a topic sentence for each section in order to create their information text (without the need to add further sentences).

Embed

Once the children have completed their notes for **Now try these** question 1, ask them to use Unit 13 Resource 2: My paragraphs to complete questions 1 and 2. Ask them to first write the topic sentences, then write additional sentences to complete their information text.

Challenge

These children can research an Olympic sport, unknown to them previously, and write a short report organising the information in paragraphs, using topic sentences.

Homework / Additional activities

Reporting an interview

Ask the children to interview members of their family about their favourite sport, hobby or interest. Children should write a short information report, using paragraphs as a way to organise the answers different people have provided.

Collins Connect: Unit 13

Ask the children to complete Unit 13 (see Teach → Year 3 → Composition → Unit 13).

Unit 14: Writing a letter

Overview

English curriculum objectives

Year 3 Children should be taught to plan their writing by:

- discussing writing similar to that which they are planning to write
- organising paragraphs around a theme
- in non-narrative material, using simple organisational devices (for example headings and subheadings).

Building towards

Children will write a letter, setting it out correctly.

Treasure House resources

- Composition Skills Pupil Book 3, Unit 14, pages 45–47

- Collins Connect Treasure House Composition Year 3, Unit 14
- Photocopiable Unit 14, Resource 1: Planning my letter, page 90
- Photocopiable Unit 14, Resource 2: My letter, page 91

Additional resources

- Stories where characters write letters (for example, *Dear Greenpeace* by Simon James) for children to browse and read
- Non-fiction examples of letters (for example, letters in newspapers, magazines) for children to browse and read

Introduction

Teaching overview

This unit focuses on how to write letters, including how to structure and lay out the contents of a letter. It also discusses the need to consider the audience and how to catch and keep the reader's attention. Children think about why letters are written, and they share any letters they know of in books they have read.

Introduce the concept

Ask children how grown-ups might communicate with a friend or family member in the present day if they lived a long way away. They will probably talk about the use of social media or email. Remind children that this has not always been so and that for many people letter writing is still a much-used method of communication.

In pairs, children should discuss what they know about letter writing: the main features and how these are set out. Take feedback and record children's ideas on an interactive whiteboard. Tell children that this unit is about letter writing.

Pupil practice

Get started

Children read the text and discuss the questions with a partner before writing their answers.

Suggested answers

1. Children discuss if they have ever written a letter before. Those that have could share this information.
2. Children discuss the details of letters they have written in the past.
3. Children discuss letters they would like to write in the future.

Try these

Children reread the text to answer questions about how to set out a letter.

Answers

1. The child correctly sets out his/her postal address. [1 mark]
2. The address should be written on the top right of the page. [1 mark]

3. You should write the date underneath the address. [1 mark]
4. A comma should come after the name of the addressee. [1 mark]
5. The letter should be organised into paragraphs. [1 mark]
6. You should sign off and write your name at the end of the letter. [1 mark]

Now try these

Children plan the content of a letter home and then write the letter.

Answers

1. Accept eight sentences on four topics that could be included in a letter. Reward imagination.
2. Accept a completed letter set out as in the example with relevant information. Reward imagination and good writing and language skills.

You may wish to use the activities and photocopiables in **Support and Embed** to give differentiated support with these activities.

Support, embed & challenge

Support

Unit 14 Resource 1: Planning my letter provides a template for a simplified version of **Now try these**. Ask the children to make notes about three things they would like to say in their letter home, before using the frame to write their letter. If helpful, ask the children to take turns to role play a phone call home before carrying out the activity.

Embed

Once the children have written their notes and initial sentences (**Now try these** question 1) ask them to write their letter (question 2) using Unit 14 Resource 2: My letter as a frame.

Challenge

Ask the children to write a letter to the head teacher about an issue they are concerned about. They could share their letters and the head teacher's response with the class.

Homework / Additional activities

Writing to a writer

Ask the children to write a real letter to an author whose books they like and to post it. Responses should be shared with the class. Alternatively, this activity could be undertaken as a joint activity by the whole class in which they collaborate on writing the letter, and discussing and agreeing on its contents.

Collins Connect: Unit 14

Ask the children to complete Unit 14 (see Teach → Year 3 → Composition → Unit 14).

Review unit 2

These tasks provide the children with the opportunity to apply and demonstrate the skills they have learned.

Explain to the children that they now have an opportunity to show their skills independently. Read through the task with the children and make sure they have understood what to do.

A. Writing a non-rhyming poem

Children copy the structure of the poem and write their own poem called 'Signs of Summer'.

Look for evidence of children's understanding of how to write a non-rhyming poem. Significant features to look out for include:

- descriptive language
- alliteration
- other poetic devices, such as onomatopoeia and personification.

B. Writing an information text

Look for evidence of children's developing understanding of how to write information texts. Significant features to look out for will include:

- an introduction and a conclusion
- use of subheadings
- a bullet-point list
- sections or paragraphs.

C. Writing instructions

Look for evidence of children's developing understanding of how to write instructions. Significant features to look out for will include:

- sequential steps set out in a list
- imperative (command) verbs
- adverbial sentence openers – for example, first, after that, next.

Unit 15: Reviewing and proofreading

Overview

English curriculum objectives

Year 3 children should be taught to:

- evaluate and edit by:
  - assessing the effectiveness of their own and others' writing and suggesting improvements
  - proposing changes to grammar and vocabulary to improve consistency, including the accurate use of pronouns in sentences.
  - proofread for spelling and punctuation errors.

Building towards

Children will write a piece of fiction writing and then review and proofread it.

Treasure House resources

- Composition Skills Pupil Book 3, Unit 15, pages 50-52
- Collins Connect Treasure House Composition Year 3, Unit 15
- Photocopiable Unit 15, Resource 1: Planet Zig, page 92
- Photocopiable Unit 15, Resource 2: The new friend, page 93

Additional resources

- A description of a character from a book the class are reading with glaring errors in punctuation, grammar, spelling and paragraphing as well as repetition of uninteresting words
- Dictionaries and thesauruses

Introduction

Teaching overview

This unit focuses on reviewing and proofreading work. The unit stresses the point that, after writing the first draft, it is necessary to check the piece for correct organisation and structure, as well as for correct punctuation and spelling.

In this unit children are provided with a character description to edit for spelling errors and are asked to create a new piece of writing, proofreading it for errors in spelling, punctuation and grammar.

Introduce the concept

Provide pairs of children with the prepared character description and ask children to review it. Ask them to discuss the ways they would improve it and then share feedback with the class. Children will likely point out:

- errors in punctuation
- errors in spelling
- errors in grammar.

Some may also suggest improvements in the structure and the use of words. Correct the piece using an interactive whiteboard, modelling the use of a dictionary and a thesaurus to correct spelling and improve vocabulary.

Finish by pointing out that reviewing their work is an important part of the composition process. Discuss with children why this is so.

Pupil practice

Pupil book pages 50–52

Get started

Children read the text and discuss the answers with a partner before writing them down.

Suggested answers

1. It is important to check work to make sure writing is organised clearly and spelling and grammar are correct.
2. Children find and discuss the errors in the example text.
3. Children look for and find errors in their writing so far this year.

Try these

Children check for spelling errors in the text provided.

Answers

Incorrect spelling		Correct spelling	
whether	[1 mark]	weather	[1 mark]
poisonus	[1 mark]	poisonous	[1 mark]
condisions	[1 mark]	conditions	[1 mark]
appeerance	[1 mark]	appearance	[1 mark]
wait	[1 mark]	weight	[1 mark]

Now try these

1. The children correct a given piece of text, writing out the corrected version.
2. The children write a description of a new alien, then rework their description, improving vocabulary before proof reading it for errors.

1. Splodge

   Splodge is also an alien. He lives near Squidge. He has won many bouncing prizes. He is blue with a red spring. He has three yellow eyes, sharp teeth and no nose. He likes to eat metal objects.

   [1 mark for each correction]

2. Accept a description of the new friend where spelling, grammar and punctuation are correct. Reward use of adventurous vocabulary.

You may wish to use the activities and photocopiables in **Support and Embed** to give differentiated support with these activities.

Support, embed & challenge

Support

Carry out **Now try these** question 1 with these children as a group task, helping the children to locate the errors. As a follow-up task, provide them with Unit 15 Resource 1: Planet Zig, which is a slightly simpler correction task, to complete in pairs. Finally, ask them to draw a picture of the new alien for question 2, label it with noun phrases and write a single sentence caption. Ask them to improve the vocabulary, then correct the spelling and punctuation of their phrases and sentence.

Embed

Ask the children to use Unit 15 Resource 2: The new friend to carry out the task described in **Now try these** question 2. They are reminded to use interesting vocabulary and to check for errors in spelling and punctuation.

Challenge

Ask these children to work in mixed-ability groups to support the proofreading of others' work.

Homework / Additional activities

Squidge and friends

Ask the children to write a story about Squidge and his friends (including their own new one). The sentences must have interesting vocabulary and be spelt and punctuated accurately. Children should be prepared to share their stories with the class and for the stories to be assessed by others, in terms of both their positives and their negatives.

Collins Connect: Unit 15

Ask the children to complete Unit 15 (see Teach → Year 3 → Composition → Unit 15).

Unit 16: Story plot

Overview

English curriculum objectives

Year 3 Children should be taught to plan their writing by:

- discussing writing similar to that which they are planning to write in order to understand and learn from its structure
- discussing and recording ideas

Year 3 children should be taught to draft and write by:

- organising paragraphs around a theme
- in narratives, creating settings, characters and plot.

Building towards

Children will develop a plot, with a clear, logical sequence of events.

Treasure House resources

- Composition Skills Pupil Book 3, Unit 16, pages 53–54
- Photocopiable Unit 16, Resource 1: Flora, page 94
- Photocopiable Unit 16, Resource 2: Developing the plot, page 95

Additional resources

- A short film or class short story
- Plots of traditional tales, with a sentence describing three–six events (for example, beginning, middle, resolution and ending) on separate pieces of paper

Introduction

Teaching overview

This unit focuses on narrative – in particular on story plot. Children will have completed units on setting, character, story openings and paragraphing and will now concentrate on developing plot. They read an extract from a short story and consider how the plot begins before working on continuing the plot or developing an alternative plot for one or more of the characters.

The extract is from a *The Black Bull*, a story by the Scottish writer Karen McCombie (born 1963), best known for her children's book series *Stella Etc. The Black Bull* is a modern variation on a traditional tale.

Introduce the concept

Watch a short film or read a short story and ask children to summarise what happened. Explain that 'what happened' is often referred to as the 'plot' and that all narratives should have (as well as character and setting) a well-planned plot.

Discuss what makes a good plot – a strong structure comprising a beginning, middle and end. Give groups of children, on separate pieces of paper, the principal events of well-known fairy tales and traditional tales (one tale per table), and ask them to place them in sequential order. Ask the children to feed back their solution to the class and to say why they think the plot should develop in that way.

Pupil practice

Get started

Children read the extract, discuss the questions with a partner and then share their answers with the class.

Suggested answers

1. The extract belongs to the beginning of a story plot. Reasons given could include the introduction of the characters and their names, the description of their home (setting) and the first mention of the characters' wishes.

2. Children talk about and share their knowledge of plots with wishes.

3. They talk about what happens to characters who make wishes.

Try these

The children reread the text and discuss the answers with a partner. Explain to the children that they will need to use their inference and prediction skills for some of the questions.

Answers

1. The story is set in a low, dark cottage by a cold, grey lake. [1 mark]

2. The family scrubbed and washed. [1 mark]

3. She wished for sons because she thought her daughters were useless. Strong sons, she felt, could help her more. [1 mark]

4. The sisters had wishes because they were fed up with their life and wanted more. [1 mark]

5. Children should write about each sister and what they think will happen to them. They might say that Kirsten leaves and has many adventures and that Mairi marries a handsome man, while Flora gets her wish to be happy. They might argue that none of the wishes come true or do so in unexpected ways. [1 mark]

Now try these

Ask the children to share their ideas of what might happen next in the story with a partner.

1. The children write the next sentence.

2. The children write a paragraph about the youngest daughter's fortunes.

3. The children write a the story of one of the other sisters and whether or not they get their wish.

Answers

1. Accept correctly punctuated sentences that are appropriate.

2. Accept paragraphs that continue the story logically. Children might develop the plot in one of two ways: the wish comes true or not.

3. They consider one of the other sisters and how the plot might develop for them.

You may wish to use the activities and photocopiables in **Support and Embed** to give differentiated support with these activities.

Support, embed & challenge

Support

Ask the children to use the structure provided by Unit 16 Resource 1: Flora complete **Now try these** questions 1 and 2. They should write sentences to accompany the storyboard. When they have finished, ask them to work with a partner to discuss ideas for question 3. Encourage them to create a short verbal story that includes some interesting or surprising events.

Embed

Once the children have completed **Now try these** questions 1 and 2, ask them to use Unit 16 Resource 2: Developing the plot to plan and write part of their story for question 3. Encourage them to create a story that contrasts with the events of the story they wrote for Flora. Remind them of the conventions of traditional tales, for example, only the youngest child or the person who wishes for the least does well and people often get exactly what they wish for (rather than what they really want – so a husband might be handsome, but boring). However, allow them to make everyone happy if they wish!

Challenge

Ask the children to devise their own plot and write four–six sentences on different pieces of paper. They can challenge a partner to sequence them.

Homework / Additional activities

Funny stories

Ask the children to remember something that happened to them or their family in the past that was funny. They should then write it as a story with a good plot!

Unit 17: Writing an information text (2)

Overview

English curriculum objectives

Children should be taught to plan their writing by:

- discussing writing similar to that which they are planning to write in order to understand and learn from its structure

Children should be taught to draft and write by:

- organising paragraphs around a theme
- in non-narrative material, using simple organisational devices [for example headings and subheadings]

Building towards

Children will write an information text in the form of a poster or fact file.

Treasure House resources

- Composition Skills Pupil Book 3, Unit 17, pages 55–56
- Photocopiable Unit 17, Resource 1: My poster, page 96
- Photocopiable Unit 17, Resource 2: My fact file, page 97

Additional resources

- A selection of non-fiction books about climate and climate change for children to browse and read

Introduction

Teaching overview

This unit focuses on writing an information text and builds on work on information texts done in Unit 11, providing an opportunity to further develop children's writing skills in this text type. The unit concentrates on presenting the information and then using it to inform or persuade the reader. It includes technical language and provides opportunities for links with the Year 3 Science and Geography curricula.

Introduce the concept

Discuss with the children what they know about climate change and read together the extract about carbon footprints in the Pupil Book. Ask the children what kind of text they have just read (non-fiction; information text) and discuss the features that make this the case.

These might include:

- the present tense
- technical vocabulary
- subheadings
- bullet lists
- definitions to help readers understand difficult words
- images (diagrams and photographs) and captions.

Pupil practice

Pupil Book pages 55–56

Get started

Children discuss the questions with a partner.

Suggested answers

1. Carbon footprint means the effect we have on the world by what we do as we burn fuel.
2. We travel and use fuel; we use electricity and gas in our homes.
3. Children provide examples of features of information texts.

Try these

Children answer questions about the information text.

Answers

1. Three examples from the following: carbon footprint, carbon dioxide, recycling, global warming. [1 mark for each]
2. A definition tells us what a technical term means. [1 mark]

3. You can find definitions of technical words in a dictionary or glossary. [1 mark]
4. You often find the present tense in an information text. [1 mark]
5. A caption tells us what a picture or diagram shows. [1 mark]

Now try these

1. Accept posters that include correct information about how to reduce our carbon footprint. Make sure children have presented the information clearly.
2. Fact files should include the relevant information and present it clearly. Children should include a bullet-point list and subheadings.

You may wish to use the activities and photocopiables in **Support and Embed** to give differentiated support with these activities.

Support, embed & challenge

Support

Ask these children to focus on **Now try these** question 1. Ask them to reread the extract in the Pupil Book and note down facts and ideas they would like to use in their poster. Encourage them to use illustrations and phrases to create their poster. Unit 17 Resource 1: My poster provides a simple template and checklist to support the children.

Embed

Ask these children to focus on **Now try these** question 2. Unit 17 Resource 2: My fact file provides a template and checklist for their writing. Remind them to use a heading, subheadings, illustrations, key words and a bullet-point list to make their fact file interesting to read. Suggest they start with the facts in the extract but enhance these with their own knowledge and further research.

Challenge

Ask these children to write an information text about climate change. They should research the issue and use their knowledge of information texts as they decide how to present the information.

Homework / Additional activities

Recycling

Ask the children to research information about recycling in their neighbourhood. Where is it collected and what can be recycled? They should write up the information and bring it to school for a class discussion.

Unit 18: Writing a rhyming poem (2)

Overview

English curriculum objectives

Reading: Year 3 children should be taught to develop positive attitudes to reading and understanding of what they read by:

- listening to and discussing a wide range of fiction and poetry
- preparing poems and play scripts to read aloud and to perform, showing understanding through intonation, tone, volume and action
- recognising some different forms of poetry (for example free verse, narrative poetry).

Writing: Year 3 children should be taught to plan their writing by discussing writing similar to that which they are planning to write in order to understand and learn from its structure.

Treasure House resources

- Composition Skills Pupil Book 3, Unit 18, pages 57–59
- Photocopiable Unit 18, Resource 1: A special memory, page 98
- Photocopiable Unit 18, Resource 2: Special memories, page 99

Additional resources

- A selection of rhyming poems, in books or online for browsing
- Specific poems with the theme of memories for children to browse and read
- A children's rhyming dictionary

Introduction

Teaching overview

This unit focuses on the use of rhyme in poetry and continues work done in Unit 8. Children read the poem 'The Old Man at My Gate' by Gareth Owen and analyse its rhyme scheme. They practise rhyming and move on to write their own rhyming poem based on the theme of memory. When they have written their poems, it is suggested that they are gathered together into a class book to share with other classes. They may also like to perform their poems in an assembly.

The subject of memory and the sharing of memories, especially by older people, such as grandparents, could be related to the PSHE curriculum.

Introduce the concept

Play some quick rhyming games, for example, ask a child to think of a word and ask another to give a rhyming word. See how far around the class you can get before the children run out of words!

Recap with children the difference between rhyming and non-rhyming poetry. Discuss which they prefer and which they find more difficult to write. Ask: 'Does having a rhyme scheme make it easier to write poems (because it provides a structure)?'

Discuss also how poems are often written around a theme or an idea. One of the themes of the poem children are about to read is memories. Explain that they will be discussing the rhyme scheme and writing their own poems on the theme of memories.

Pupil practice

Pupil Book pages 57–59

Get started

Children read the poem with a partner, discuss the structure of the poem and feed back their answers to the class.

Answers

1. There are three stanzas of four lines each.

2. Each line begins with a capital letter (even if it isn't necessarily the start of a new sentence). (Be prepared to discuss that this is a convention, one not always used.)

3. The second and fourth lines rhyme. The first and third do not.

4. For example: An old man visits the house he used to live in, remembers playing football in the street with his friends and wishes he could return to that time.

Try these

The children reread the poem and use the questions to investigate and respond to the poem. Afterwards, discuss the children's responses to the poem and whether they liked it or not. Discuss the theme, discussing memory and introducing the word 'nostalgia'.

Suggested answers

1. The children complete the first two columns of the table: gate/late; ago/know; more/shore. They should provide another rhyming word for each row.
[1 mark for each rhyming pair]

2. The children add more rhyming words to complete the table. [1 mark per new rhyming word]

3. The poet uses a strong rhythm. [1 mark]

4. The children should say why they like or dislike the poem, explaining with reference to the poem or how it makes them feel.

5. Accept any suitable answer, for example: memory, regret about time passing.

Now try these

1. Children make a list of three special memories and choose one as the subject of a four-line stanza, following the rhyme scheme in the Pupil Book poem.

2. Accept two more stanzas following the same rhyme scheme.

You may wish to use the activities and photocopiables in **Support and Embed** to give differentiated support with these activities.

Support, embed & challenge

Support

Ask these children to focus on **Now try these** question 1. Encourage them to discuss their memory in pairs first, then note down some noun phrases and rhyming words they could use. Ask the children to use the structure provided in Unit 18 Resource 1: A special memory to support them as they write a four-line poem called 'A Special Memory'.

Embed

Ask these children to use Unit 18 Resource 2: Special memories to write their stanzas for **Now try these** questions 1 and 2. Encourage them to share their

memories with a partner before they start to help them focus on which part of each memory is special and interesting. Once they've written a first version of the poem on the resource sheet, ask them to share their poem with a partner, who should suggest better vocabulary and spot any spelling mistakes. Ask the children to write an improved final version on a new sheet of paper.

Challenge

Ask these children to write their own rhyming poem, using a rhyme scheme of their choice, based on their memories of starting school.

Homework / Additional activities

Memory poem

Ask the children to interview their parents and/or grandparents about any special memories they have from when they were younger. Together they write a short rhyming poem based on these memories. They should be prepared to read their poems out to the class.

Unit 19: Writing an explanation text

Overview

English curriculum objectives

Year 3 Children should be taught to plan their writing by:

- discussing writing similar to that which they are planning to write in order to understand and learn from its structure.

Year 3 children should be taught to draft and write by:

- in non-narrative material, using simple organisational devices (for example, headings and subheadings).

Building towards

Children will write an explanation text about how a kite works.

Treasure House resources

- Composition Skills Pupil Book 3, Unit 19, pages 60–62
- Photocopiable Unit 19, Resource 1: Labelled flowchart, page 100
- Photocopiable Unit 19, Resource 2: Flowchart with sentences, page 101

Additional resources

- A selection of non-fiction books about how things work for children to browse and read
- A few yo-yos for children to play with and observe how they work and/or a short film clip of someone playing with a yo-yo
- A short film clip showing how a kite works

Introduction

Teaching overview

This unit focuses on writing an explanation text. It concentrates on explaining the process and structuring a text. The extract is taken from *How Does It Work?* and, after reading how a yo-yo works and learning about the features of an explanation text, the children are asked to explain how a kite works with the use of a flowchart. This work on learning the skills of writing explanatory text is useful for cross-curricular work in Science and could be carried out in conjunction with teaching about forces (gravity).

Introduce the concept

If possible, have some yo-yos for children to use. Ask if anyone knows what a yo-yo is and if anyone has ever played with one. If it is not possible to bring a yo-yo in, look for a short film clip to show to the children. Ask if they have any idea how it works and to share those ideas with a partner. Allow the children to use the yo-yos to help them. Invite the children to feed back their ideas to the class.

Tell children that the unit will examine how to write explanatory text, including the use of numbered lists, flowcharts and diagrams.

Move on to discuss how a kite works. Ask the children to share experiences of kite flying and, together, watch a video that explains the process simply. Recap on how a kite flies ensuring that the children understand (a simple version of) the process.

Pupil practice

Pupil Book pages 60–62

Get started

Children read the text and discuss their answers with a partner.

Suggested answers

1. Children discuss if they have ever played with a yo-yo and attempt to explain how one works.

2. For example: The kite is thrown up into the air with a force greater then its weight. This keeps the kite travelling until it catches the wind. The wind lifts the kite until the string is tight. The wind travels over and under the kite, keeping it in the air. The string stops the kite flying away.

3. They begin to discuss what is needed to explain to someone how something works (for example, use of the present tense; a numbered list; a diagram). (There will be more on this as they read through the Pupil Book.)

Try these

Children answer questions about information texts.

Answers

1. An explanation text may begin with a description of the object. [1 mark]

2. Diagrams are often included. [1 mark]

3. Labels tell you the names of the different parts of the object. [1 mark]

4. A list is included because it describes how something works in a logical order. [1 mark]

5. A fun or interesting fact often goes into a box. [1 mark]

6. The present tense is used. [1 mark]

Now try these

1. Children draw a series of labelled diagrams to explain how a kite works.

2. They move on to adding full sentences to explain the process.

Answers

1. Accept flowcharts that show the process in a sequential order, labelled correctly.

2. Accept explanations that are in a sequential order, explained in full sentences using the present tense.

You may wish to use the activities and photocopiables in **Support and Embed** to give differentiated support with these activities.

Support, embed & challenge

Support

Ask these children to focus on **Now try these** question 1, aiming to create a clear explanation in the form of a series of labelled diagrams. Ask the children to use the flowchart provided on Unit 19 Resource 1: Labelled flowchart to draw their series of diagrams to show the process of how a kite works. They should add labels to each part of the flowchart.

Embed

Ask these children to use Unit 19 Resource 2: Flowchart with sentences to write their explanation text for **Now try these**. Ask them to first draw a series of four labelled diagrams (question 1) before adding full sentence explanations to accompany each diagram. Remind them to use the present tense.

Challenge

Ask these children to create a poster explaining how a kite works, using as many information text features as they can. They could work on this in pairs or small groups.

Homework / Additional activities

How a boomerang works

Ask the children to research information about what a boomerang is and how it works. They should then draw a flowchart explaining the process.

Unit 20: Writing recounts

Overview

English curriculum objectives

Year 3 Children should be taught to plan their writing by:

- discussing writing similar to that which they are planning to write
- organising paragraphs around a theme
- in narratives, creating settings, characters and plot
- in non-narrative material, using simple organisational devices (for example headings and subheadings).

Treasure House resources

- Composition Skills Pupil Book 3, Unit 20, pages 63–65
- Photocopiable Unit 20, Resource 1: The Great Fire of London, page 102
- Photocopiable Unit 20, Resource 2: My history recount, page 103

Additional resources

- Selection of history texts – some about the Great Fire of London and some linked to the class's current history topic – for children to browse and read
- A short film about the Great Fire of London

Introduction

Teaching overview

This unit focuses on developing children's understanding of the features of a recount text. It uses an extract from an account of the Great Fire of London. Children are asked to recount the events that supposedly caused the beginnings of the fire in a short paragraph. You will need to ensure that children's knowledge of verbs in the past tense is secure.

Recounts often use storytelling devices (such as a sequential narrative in the past tense) to inform readers about a non-fiction event. They are therefore useful for writing about historical events.

The Great Fire of London largely destroyed the medieval City of London: more than 13 000 houses and 87 churches were burned to the ground. Some 70 000 Londoners were left homeless. It is not known how many people died. The fire was followed by a massive rebuilding programme that saw the birth of London as it is today.

Introduce the concept

Show children a short film clip about the Great Fire of London and then ask them to say what happened in the fire. Point out that when we do this we do so using the past tense of a verb. Ask children to retell an event they know about from their current history topic. Point out that when we retell an event from the past we call that written text a recount.

Tell children that they will read an extract from a short recount of the Fire of London in 1666. They will then write a recount of the start of the fire and move on to write their own recount of an event from history known to them.

Pupil practice

Pupil Book pages 63–65

Get started

Children read the extract and discuss their answers with a partner.

Suggested answers

1. The word 'tinder' is normally used to refer to any material, like dry grass, wood, straw, and so on that can be used to start a fire quickly. In the old days, every home had a tinderbox. It was a small metal box that contained tinder and all the other things required to light a fire. When London is described as a 'tinderbox', it means that, if it were to catch fire, it would burn down very quickly.

2. For example, past tense verbs, events told in order, explains who, what, where and when, sometimes pictures with captions, paragraphs and 'time' words.

3. Children give reasons why they can tell they are reading a non-fiction text – the use of precise dates and settings; the use of technical language; the description of causes and effects; the use of captions. Afterwards, explain that, generally, history recounts rely on evidence to tell their story.

Try these

Children answer questions about the extract and recounts.

Answers

1. Recounts are useful for writing about events in the past, especially history. [1 mark]

2. The time and setting are often given at the beginning of a recount. [1 mark]

3. The word 'went' is the past tense. [1 mark]

4. Children can draw from a range of verbs in the past tense, including: were, built, kept, helped, touched, crowded, destroyed, went, stacked. [1 mark per verb]

5. A caption tells us what a picture shows. [1 mark]

Now try these

1. The children use the information in the extract, the discussion and information shared in the introduction to the lesson and any other research they are able to do, to write a recount of the events at Pudding Lane from the baker's actions to the fire starting and beginning to spread.

2. The children use the extract as a model to write a recount about another historical event they have studied.

Suggested answers

1. Accept a recount where the events are written in sequential order and in the past tense.

2. Accept recounts that 'retell' the event the child has chosen in sequential order and using the past tense. The recount should also include interesting details.

You may wish to use the activities and photocopiables in **Support and Embed** to give differentiated support with these activities.

Support, embed & challenge

Support

Organise for these children to focus on **Now try these** question 1. Recap with them the events of the first night of the Great Fire of London, working together to ensure all the children can verbally retell the events in question before they start to write. Unit 20 Resource 1: The Great Fire of London provides a template for them to use as they write an illustrated recount of the night covering three events.

Embed

Once the children have completed **Now try these** question 1, help them to choose a new historical event to recount in question 2, providing access to books and the internet to allow them to research and check facts. Unit 20 Resource 2: My history recount provides a simple template for them to use as they write their recount.

Challenge

Ask the children to research further information about the Great Fire of London and to write a full recount of how it spread, how it ended and what happened afterwards.

Homework / Additional activities

Recounting a school event

Ask the children to choose an event at school, possibly an outing or trip, to recount in writing. Once written, it can be shared with the class.

Review unit 3

These tasks provide the children with the opportunity to apply and demonstrate the skills they have learned.

Explain to the children that they now have an opportunity to show their skills independently. Read through the task with the children and make sure they have understood what to do.

A. Writing a letter

Look for evidence of children's understanding of how to write an informal letter. Significant features to look out for include:

- correctly set out postal address, written in the top right of the page
- date written underneath the address
- a comma after the name of the addressee
- organised into paragraphs
- name of sender written at the end of the letter after the sign-off.

B. Paragraphs in non-fiction

Look for evidence of children's developing understanding of how to write paragraphs in non-fiction. Significant features to look out for include:

- four to five sentences in each paragraph
- paragraphs starting on a new line
- a new paragraph beginning with an indent
- use of a topic sentence to start each new paragraph.

C. Writing explanations

Look for evidence of children's developing understanding of how to write explanatory text. Significant features to look out for include:

- technical vocabulary
- verbs in the present tense
- sequential order of the process possibly shown in a flowchart.

My flowchart

Plan your story by completing the flowchart.
Add your ideas to each section.

The story begins

The build-up to a problem

The problem

Characters solve the problem

The story ends

Story opening

Use these boxes to plan your story opening.

Main character

Three things about the main character

Second character

Setting

Three things at the setting

Now write the first paragraph of your story. Introduce the setting and the main character. Write four or five sentences.

_____

_____

_____

_____

_____

_____

My three story settings

Draw three different settings. Label the settings with descriptive noun phrases (for example: *A wild, lonely forest*).

Setting 1

Setting 2

Setting 3

Choose one setting and write a descriptive sentence about it.

_____

_____

My story setting

Choose a setting and describe it. Bring it to life for the reader through descriptive phrases and details of the sights and sounds.

My setting

_____

_____

_____

_____

_____

_____

_____

_____

_____

When you have finished writing the description, draw an illustration of the scene.

Reporting words

Write a list of reporting words here.

These are words to use instead of 'said' when you are writing speech.

1. _____

2. _____

3. _____

4. _____

5. _____

Now write a sentence with dialogue for each reporting word. For example: "What big ears you have, Grandma!" **exclaimed** Little Red Riding Hood.

1. _____

2. _____

3. _____

4. _____

5. _____

A dialogue between Mr Baxter and his friend

Write a paragraph where Mr Baxter tells his friend about his new bow tie.

Use these prompts to help you remember how to punctuate dialogue.

1. Put speech marks at the start and end of spoken word.

2. Put a capital letter at the start of the speech.

3. Start a new line for each new speaker.

4. Punctuate the speech before the closing speech marks.

5. Try to vary the reporting words you use.

_____

_____

_____

_____

_____

_____

_____

_____

_____

_____

_____

_____

Story openings – sentences

Write different story opening sentences. The first one has been done for you.

Story opening 1 – dialogue

"And what have we got to remember to bring tomorrow?" Mrs Cooper asked.

Story opening 2 – setting

Story opening 3 – character

Story opening 4 – question

Story openings – paragraph

Think about the different ways of opening a story and choose your favourite.

Write the opening to a story using the method you have chosen. It should consist of three or four sentences.

_____

_____

_____

_____

Use the space below to plan how the rest of your story will develop. You could draw a story map or a flowchart of your ideas.

Write the next paragraph in your story. Remember to keep the reader interested!

_____

_____

_____

_____

My character

Draw a picture of your character in the space below. Add noun phrases (for example, *A tall, lanky boy*) to describe what they look like. Give your character a name.

Write a sentence about what kinds of things your character likes to do.

_____

_____

Write a sentence that your character might say.

_____

_____

Planning my character's story

Draw a picture of your character here.

Draw the setting for the story.

What is going to happen to your character in the story you have invented…

at the beginning?

_____

_____

in the middle?

_____

_____

at the end?

_____

_____

Continuing a story: King Arthur

Use the storyboard to write your story about what happens next to Arthur. Your story begins:

Arthur then became King.

Draw a picture here.	Write the story.
	_____ _____ _____ _____ _____ _____
Draw a picture here.	Write the story.
	_____ _____ _____ _____ _____ _____
Draw a picture here.	Write the story.
	_____ _____ _____ _____ _____ _____

Continuing a story: Merlin

Merlin has heard about what has happened to Arthur.
Continue the story below. Think about what he might
do and how he would want to protect Arthur.

_____

_____

_____

_____

_____

_____

_____

Illustrate your story here.

My new paragraph

Read the story 'Shadow'. Think about what might happen next.
Write the next paragraph. Think about why this is a new
paragraph. Have you changed the setting? Are you introducing
a new character? Is the action happening at a different time?
Underneath, draw an illustration of your new paragraph.

Paragraph checklist

You are writing a checklist for next year's Year 3 class.
The checklist is about the use of paragraphs and you
have to explain to the new class what the rules are for using paragraphs.
If you want to show some examples, use the story 'Shadow'.

My rhyming poem

Write a poem with the same rhyming pattern as in 'Water'.

Call your poem 'Snow' or 'The Sun'.

Line 1 (Rhymes with line 3)

_____

_____

_____

Line 2 (Rhymes with line 4)

_____

_____

_____

Line 3 (Rhymes with line 1)

_____

_____

_____

Line 4 (Rhymes with line 2)

_____

_____

_____

My season poem

Write a poem with six lines where line 1 rhymes with line 2, line 3 rhymes with line 4, and line 5 rhymes with line 6.

Write about your favourite season.

Line 1 (Rhymes with line 2)

Line 2 (Rhymes with line 1)

Line 3 (Rhymes with line 4)

Line 4 (Rhymes with line 3)

Line 5 (Rhymes with line 6)

Line 6 (Rhymes with line 5)

My descriptive phrases

Draw pictures of three scenes you might see from your window in winter.

Draw a picture here.	Describe the scene.
	_____
	_____
	_____
	_____
	_____
	_____
Draw a picture here.	Describe the scene.
	_____
	_____
	_____
	_____
	_____
	_____
Draw a picture here.	Describe the scene.
	_____
	_____
	_____
	_____
	_____
	_____
	_____

From my window

Write a non-rhyming poem about looking through a window in winter. Each verse should describe a different scene.

Use the list to check the techniques you have used.

Checklist of poetic techniques you could use:

- descriptive language
- alliteration

- onomatopoeia
- personification

Write your poem here.

Verse 1

_____

_____

_____

_____

Verse 2

_____

_____

_____

_____

Verse 3

_____

_____

_____

_____

Planning my report

Plan your non-fiction report by completing the spider diagram.
Add your ideas to each section.

Where does my creature live?

What does my creature eat?

Name of creature

What does my creature look like?

Illustration

My report

Introduce your chosen creature here.

_____

_____

_____

Write your report here. Remember to include subheadings as you organise the different pieces of information into sections.

_____

_____

_____

_____

_____

_____

_____

_____

Write your conclusion or summary here.

_____

_____

_____

_____

_____

_____

_____

_____

Planning my report

Title of my information report:

_____

Section 1 – subheading

_____

_____

Section 2 – subheading

_____

_____

Section 3 – subheading

_____

_____

Section 4 – subheading

_____

_____

Checklist
• Have you included an introduction and conclusion? • Have you included a bullet-point list?

My report

Title of my information report:

_____

Write your information report here. Use the checklist provided.

_____

_____

_____

_____

_____

_____

_____

_____

_____

_____

_____

_____

_____

Checklist

- Have you included an introduction?

- Have you organised the information into sections?

- Do the sections have subheadings?

- Have you included a bullet-point list?

- Have you checked for core punctuation?

Getting ready to cook

The food item I am making is _____.

Draw a picture of what it will look like.

Equipment I will need: (write a list)

_____

_____

_____

_____

_____

Draw pictures of the equipment.

Ingredients I will need: (write a list)

_____

_____

_____

_____

_____

Draw pictures of the ingredients.

My recipe

Write a list of instructions for how to make your food item.

Include labelled diagrams. Check for imperative verbs.
Add more steps if you need to.

1	
2	
3	
4	
5	

My topic sentences

My sport/hobby/interest

_____

Paragraph 1: Topic sentence

_____

_____

Paragraph 2: Topic sentence

_____

_____

Paragraph 3: Topic sentence

_____

_____

Paragraph 4: Topic sentence

_____

_____

Paragraph 5: Topic sentence

_____

_____

My paragraphs

My sport/hobby/interest

_____

Paragraph 1: Topic sentence _____

Additional sentences _____

_____

_____

Paragraph 2: Topic sentence _____

Additional sentences _____

_____

_____

Paragraph 3: Topic sentence _____

Additional sentences _____

_____

_____

Paragraph 4: Topic sentence _____

Additional sentences _____

_____

_____

Paragraph 5: Topic sentence _____

Additional sentences _____

_____

_____

Planning my letter

What information will I include in my letter home?

1. _____

2. _____

3. _____

My draft letter:

Dear _____ ,

I am writing to tell you about _____

While I was there I _____

_____

_____

_____

_____

_____

Love from _____

Draw an illustration of your visit or outing.

My letter

(Write your name and postal address here.)

(Write the date here.)

(Name of person you are writing to)

(Write the paragraphs of your letter here.)

(Sign your letter here.)

Planet Zig

planet Zig is verry big. It has manny moones they circle the planet.
there ar craters on the surfiss the air is poisonus it is always drk their.
no plants liv on zig but squidge and Splodge luv it

Write the corrected description of Planet Zig here. You can add an illustration of the planet when you have finished.

© HarperCollins*Publishers* 2017

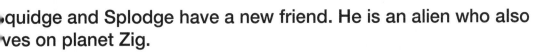

The new friend

Squidge and Splodge have a new friend. He is an alien who also lives on planet Zig.

Write a description of their new friend using interesting words.
Check your spelling and punctuation.

_____

_____

_____

_____

_____

_____

_____

_____

When you have finished you may draw a picture of their new friend here.

Flora

Write the next sentence in the story.

_____

_____

What happens to Flora? How does her story develop?

_____

_____

Draw a picture here.	Write the story.
	_____
	_____
	_____
	_____
	_____
Draw a picture here.	Write the story.
	_____
	_____
	_____
	_____
	_____
Draw a picture here.	Write the story.
	_____
	_____
	_____
	_____
	_____

Developing the plot

Choose one of the other characters in the story.
How does their story develop?

Draw a picture here.	Write notes for the story.
Draw a picture here.	Write notes for the story.
Draw a picture here.	Write notes for the story.

Write the first paragraph in full in this space.

My poster

Checklist

- Have you included all the information the reader will need?

- Have you included a bullet-point list?

- Have you used illustrations or diagrams?

My fact file

Title of my fact file

What is a carbon footprint?

Insert your definition here.

Add illustrations.

How can we help to reduce our carbon footprint?

Insert your bullet-point list here.

Add illustrations.

Check that you have organised the information using subheadings.

Add any further illustrations or ideas of your own here.

A special memory

Write a poem with the same rhyming pattern as in 'The Old Man at My Gate'. It should be about a special memory you have.

A Special Memory

Line 1

_____

Line 2 (rhymes with line 4)

_____

Line 3

_____

Line 4 (rhymes with line 2)

_____

Draw a picture to illustrate your poem

Special memories

Write a poem with three verses about special memories you have. It should have the same rhyming pattern as 'The Old Man at My Gate'.

Stanza 1

_____

_____

_____

_____

_____

Stanza 2

_____

_____

_____

_____

Stanza 3

_____

_____

_____

_____

Labelled flowchart

Add pictures to the flowchart to explain how a kite works. Add labels to go with each illustration.

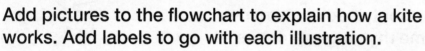

Flowchart with sentences

Draw a flowchart to explain how a kite works.

Add sentences to each part of the flowchart explaining what is happening in the process.

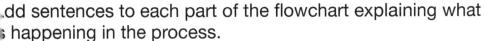

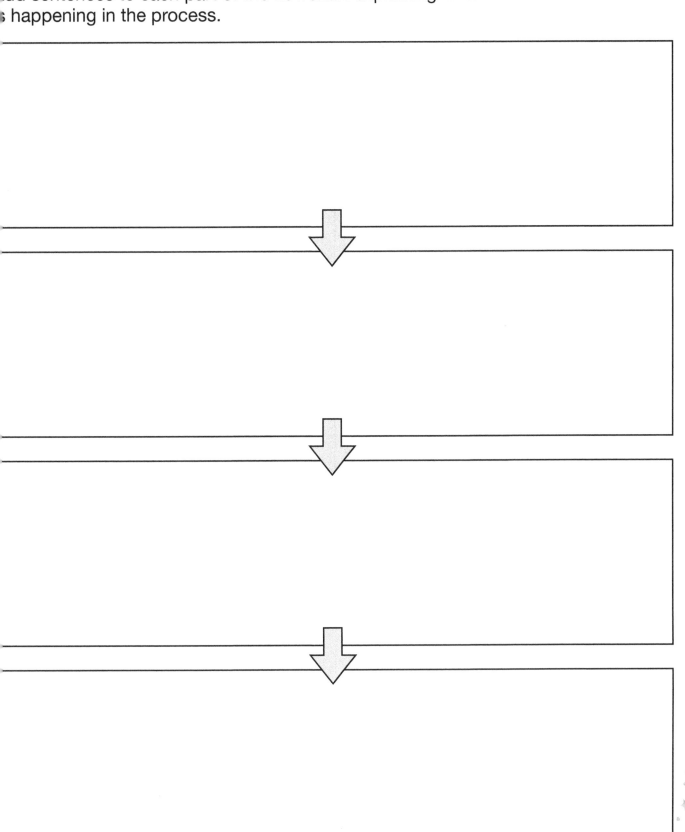

The Great Fire of London

Write a paragraph recounting what happened in
Pudding Lane at the start of the fire.

Add more boxes if you need them.

Draw a picture here.	Write the story.
	_____ _____ _____ _____ _____ _____
Draw a picture here.	Write the story. _____ _____ _____ _____ _____ _____
Draw a picture here.	Write the story. _____ _____ _____ _____ _____ _____

My history recount

Write a recount of the history event you have chosen.
Use the checklist provided.

_____

_____

_____

_____

_____

_____

_____

Illustrate your recount when you have finished.

Checklist

• Write in the past tense.

• Write about the event in the order in which things happened.

• Include interesting details.